Michael P Ward

The Telescope

A Familiar Sketch, Combining a Special Notice of Objects Coming Within the Range

of a Small Telescope. Third Edition

Michael P Ward

The Telescope
A Familiar Sketch, Combining a Special Notice of Objects Coming Within the Range of a Small Telescope. Third Edition

ISBN/EAN: 9783337139643

Printed in Europe, USA, Canada, Australia, Japan

Cover: Foto ©Andreas Hilbeck / pixelio.de

More available books at **www.hansebooks.com**

THE TELESCOPE:

A FAMILIAR SKETCH

COMBINING

A SPECIAL NOTICE OF OBJECTS COMING WITHIN THE RANGE OF A

SMALL TELESCOPE,

WITH A

DETAIL OF THE MOST INTERESTING DISCOVERIES WHICH HAVE BEEN
MADE WITH THE ASSISTANCE OF POWERFUL TELESCOPES,

CONCERNING THE

PHENOMENA OF THE HEAVENLY BODIES.

BY

THE HON. MRS. WARD.

ILLUSTRATED BY THE AUTHOR'S ORIGINAL DRAWINGS.

THIRD EDITION.

LONDON:
GROOMBRIDGE AND SONS,
5, PATERNOSTER ROW.
―
MDCCCLXIX.

PRINTED BY J. E. ADLARD,
BARTHOLOMEW CLOSE.

TO

THE EARL OF ROSSE.

IN thanking you for the permission which you have kindly given me to dedicate to you this little book on Astronomy, I am reminded that my earliest attempts to observe the wonders of the heavens were made in consequence of your having, many years ago, commended the two-inch Telescope in my possession as being good, so far as its limited powers extended. I have now gratefully to record a somewhat similar verdict which you have given in favour of these pages, encouraging my hope that some who read them may be led by their perusal to study and observe for themselves the wonders which I have endeavoured to describe. But I am aware that anything which I can offer is as much exceeded by the scientific treatment of which the subject is capable, as my two-inch Dollond is surpassed by that noble and unrivalled TELESCOPE, with which some of my happiest recollections are associated.

M. W.

TRIMLESTON HOUSE, NEAR DUBLIN.

CONTENTS.

CHAPTER I.
The Observer's Apparatus, and what to observe

CHAPTER II.
The Sun . . . . .

CHAPTER III.
The Earth . . . . .

CHAPTER IV.
The Moon . . . . .

CHAPTER V.
Eclipses of the Sun and Moon . .

CHAPTER VI.
Mercury and Venus . . . .

CHAPTER VII.

	PAGE
MARS	71

CHAPTER VIII.

JUPITER	77

CHAPTER IX.

SATURN	86

CHAPTER X.

COMETS	92

CHAPTER XI.

SHOOTING STARS AND OTHER LUMINOUS METEORS	116

CHAPTER XII.

FIXED STARS	122

CHAPTER XIII.

CLUSTERS OF STARS AND NEBULÆ	143

PREFACE.

CAN Astronomy be presented as an entertaining study? Has any one attempted to cull from treatises addressed to the not wholly unlearned in science, facts, and anecdotes, the "light literature" of this sublime study, and to tell these things in simple words?

And to give the interest of *reality* to these facts, has it been suggested to those who can admire and wonder at the splendour of the firmament, to try how much they can improve their view of star or planet, by examining them with the help of a small telescope, such as one may see, perchance, at every sixth window, on a fine summer's day, at a watering-place, its object-glass, capable of better things, idly directed to fishing-boat or distant steamer, or still more idly, to unconscious group on the pier?

As we believe that these attempts, namely, to relate a few of the discoveries of the learned, in words which the unlearned can understand, and to tell how much may be seen of the heavenly bodies with a small telescope, have not been hitherto combined, we now venture on the task.

This little book does not attempt to teach Astronomy, it deals principally with observation; showing how the stars appear in their season, coming back year after year in their appointed time, while the stately planets move in their solemn paths, changing their places gradually among the unchanging stars, as they have done before our time, and will do when we have passed away.

Happy should we be could we impart the very great pleasure which even this humble form of Astronomy can give. The warm interest, the almost personal affection that can be felt for the well-known planet, the familiar constellation, the double star that has been scanned with the little telescope is no matter of speculation with the author of this slight treatise. The delight at the first appearance in the autumn of glorious Orion, seen by chance at midnight, the satisfaction when Jupiter is again descried, after being some months concealed by the neighbourhood of the Sun's beams, are feelings yearly experienced by us, and little influenced by time, place, or even by circumstances. From foreign lands, from crowded cities, from the open windows of our quiet home, from the silent road leading from some scene of festivity, they are seen with nearly the same thoughts and feelings. They seem like friends. The distant planets are the solemn way-marks of the years that have passed since we first observed their positions; the southern horizon hides from our view a firmament unseen by us, but nightly spread over those we know and love in distant lands. The faint comet-like spots that appear to our eyes when accustomed to the darkness, are clusters of stars, discernible even through our little telescope. But what of that wondrous belt which traverses the sky,— the Milky Way? Our eyes and our little instrument are alike unable to decipher it; but as we look on it we remember what has been revealed about it by a powerful telescope, namely this, "that it consists "entirely of stars scattered by millions, like glittering dust, on the black ground of the general heavens."[*] Stars—each, perhaps, a Sun! Far, far away from this earth and its troubles is the mind carried by such thoughts and remembrances. And still farther may it be uplifted in this quiet hour, even to the throne of Him whom the heaven of heavens cannot contain, but who yet looks so lovingly on his creature man, from the place of his habitation.

"He healeth the broken in heart, and bindeth up their wounds.

He telleth the number of the stars; he calleth them ALL by their names."—Psa. cxlvii. 3, 4.

[*] Herschel's 'Treatise on Astronomy,' p. 163.

THE TELESCOPE.

CHAPTER I.

THE OBSERVER'S APPARATUS; AND, WHAT TO OBSERVE.

TO point out how we may see for ourselves, and to relate a little of what has been observed by others;—these are the objects of this little book.

The latter will be attempted in succeeding chapters, and the former will form the subject of the present one.

We will suppose the reader, already interested in the appearance of the starry heavens, and acquainted, perhaps, with one or two constellations, inquiring how he may learn more, and what apparatus will be necessary for making observations.

We would answer, you should have a set of *maps of the stars*, an *Almanack* with tables of the positions of the planets, and other astronomical information, and *a telescope which you can fix steadily*; we will suppose it is a good telescope, but with an object-glass only two inches in diameter,* or even less. If you are privileged

* Technically known as "two inches in *aperture*."

to use a more powerful instrument at any future time, you will value it all the more from having first learned to work with a small telescope.

We have indicated the apparatus in the order which it is most desirable that the beginner should observe in using them.

First, the maps, by means of which you by degrees become acquainted with the relative position of the various stars, and in consequence able to detect the progress amongst them of one of those wandering stars, the five visible *planets*.

Second, the almanack, which directs the observer already instructed in the bearings of the stars, where to expect and find any given planet.

Third, the telescope, to scan the stars now familiar, and therefore additionally interesting, and to observe the planets which have been identified.

But we do not forbid the learner to reverse this order occasionally, long before the maps are mastered, and while the columns of the almanack still seem little better than a dull array of figures. He may lawfully encourage himself in his studies by looking through the telescope, pointing at random to one of the brilliant specks which he fancies may be a planet from its calm steady light. It may chance to be a discovery to him that the same telescope which enables him to read the name of a merchant brig at half a mile's distance, is also able to make the difference between a star and a planet strikingly apparent.

The planet Saturn is, while I am observing it, in a part of the heavens not far removed, in apparent position, from the stars Castor and Pollux, or Procyon in the constellation of "the little Dog," and to the unassisted eye is very similar to that star. But turn the telescope to each in succession; Procyon appears a brilliant diamond point, how very bright and sparkling, but how small! Now let us see Saturn; behold! there is the very planet of the astronomy books, with its round disc like a tiny moon, and its broad brilliant ring. Perhaps the seldom-used night eye-piece in the telescope-case (discarded long ago, because it turned the name of the merchant brig upside down, though it did make the letters somewhat larger), may improve our view of the planet. We screw it on, removing the day eye-piece, and we can now plainly see Saturn's shadow thrown on the brilliant surface of its ring, and can faintly descry its satellite "Titan" (Plate VIII). They look very small, it is true, but the feeling that now indeed we *see* an object of which hitherto we had only *heard*, is always vividly experienced at a first sight of Saturn. The *beauty*, too, of the real planet never fails to strike the beholder in a way no pictured representation can. Possibly the reader exclaims here, "I wish I had any idea where to find Saturn, or that I even knew Castor and Pollux, and the little Dog." Then study your maps, and before long no large star visible in our latitude will be a stranger to you. We recommend maps rather than a globe for the purpose of learning the stars, for two plain practical reasons; one is, that on the globe the stars are turned the contrary way, appearing as they would in a looking-glass, which arrangement, though necessary when the concave firmament is represented as if viewed from outside, is very confusing to a beginner. The other reason in favour of maps is that they are portable. The observer, well wrapped up, at an open window, or fairly in the open air, can so easily carry about a thin book of maps, and studying for awhile by lantern-light some one group of stars represented in it, at once turn his eyes to the stars themselves, till the same group is found and its position committed to the memory.*

A plain distinct set of maps, such as one would not mind half wearing out in the service, is much the best to learn with. The only set which the author ever used were those of Middleton's Celestial Atlas. In this work the stars visible in Great Britain are represented in five pages, engraved in the usual manner, with the lines of right ascension and declination, the equator and ecliptic, and the pictured figures of the constellations; each page being faced by a *blank map*, in which the stars are vividly represented in white, on a black ground, and corresponding exactly in size and position to those on the "illustrated" page.

* A Planisphere will also be found very useful. This is an ingenious arrangement of three discs of pasteboard, by means of which all the principal stars visible in Great Britain at any given day and hour will be indicated, and the times of their rising and setting clearly pointed out.

The same information may be obtained (we need scarcely say) by a simple problem on the celestial globe; but for the mere purpose of studying the face of the heavens, the cheap and portable Planisphere is preferable. The beautiful precision and ingenious arrangements of a good celestial globe become, however, a source of great pleasure to those who have by a little persevering attention, made themselves acquainted with the actual movements of the heavens.

The advantage of this plan consists in the blank map being unencumbered with lines, figures, or names of any kind, and in its simplicity and vivid contrast of black and white bearing a resemblance to the starry firmament which it represents. The names and positions of the stars can at once be ascertained by referring to the neighbouring page.

Very lately we have met with a *popular* guide to the constellations, in which this plan of clear and simple maps form a prominent feature.* It is of small quarto size, and seems peculiarly well adapted for the purpose of teaching the constellations gradually, to persons hitherto acquainted with very few or with none of them; and with a second atlas of the heavens, by the same author,† in which all the constellations are represented in four large and correct maps, would, if carefully studied on favorable evenings, *from month to month,* make the student thoroughly acquainted with every remarkable group, and each bright star in the glowing firmament.

We have endeavoured to attract the reader's especial attention to the circumstance that the stars visible in this latitude cannot all be seen in the course of one night; and we now wish to state the facts of the case, and, if possible, to state them so plainly that the reader may *really know* how the stars appear to move.

We will suppose, reader, that with regard to the

---

* 'An Easy Guide to the Constellations, with a Miniature Atlas of the Stars, and Key Maps.' By James Gall, jun.

† 'The People's Atlas of the Stars, with Key Maps; being a companion to the Easy Guide to the Constellations.'

movements of the heavenly bodies, you know but one fact with absolute clearness and certainty, namely, that the Sun rises every day in the east, glorious and glowing from behind the horizon, and travels southwards in a sloping direction till about noon, and that, as the day goes on, he evidently travels downwards, and at last sinks behind the western horizon, leaving only radiant clouds to tell of his brightness; and that the twilight gives way to night, and again, after some hours, night to twilight, and the Sun rises again. Nay, dear reader, be not offended at this low estimate of your knowledge; we speak only of what you know with absolute clearness and certainty, and what you have had so many more opportunities of observing than you are likely to have enjoyed with regard to the fixed stars. For how few have followed in the track of the Chaldean shepherds, they who were among the earliest to collect and hand down to succeeding ages the facts of astronomy!

Did our usual occupations, like theirs, call us to spend *the whole night* under the blue vault of heaven, we should soon see for ourselves, and thoroughly comprehend, that even as the Sun rises in the east, travels upwards to the south, and descends in the west, so do all the stars which we can see as we sit to watch them, facing the south, the direction where the Sun was at noon.

All the night through we should observe that there are stars rising above the horizon at our left, others drifting slowly along opposite to us, others sinking at our right. We might also perceive that those which rise but a little way eastward of the south point which we are facing, remain but a short time in our view, never rise to any great height, and set but a little way west of the southern point of the horizon, and then remain invisible for many hours. Whereas those which rise so far to the east that we must look exactly over our left shoulder to see them emerge above the horizon, rise to a great height overhead, set far to the west, and remain so long in sight (namely, twelve hours), that the morning twilight has almost come before they have sunk at our right hand.

The stars still further removed from the south quarter of the horizon, what of them? They are still longer above the horizon, and a shorter time below than those that rise in the east. Turning our eyes completely away from the southern to the northern horizon, what do we see? Stars which merely descend for a brief interval, and again ascend; and above them, stars which never set at all, but slowly revolve round the almost stationary Pole Star.

But neither our present business, or we might say, the business of this little book, is with these northern stars, which indeed revolve like the others, but cannot be said to rise or set, as they are perpetually in sight on every cloudless night. We again turn our eyes to the south, and endeavour to impress on the reader that if he spent the whole of one clear night in the open air, he would see stars rising and setting, as he sees the Sun do by day. Or, without rivalling the Chaldean astronomers by actually watching all night, he may prove the same thing by observing the rising of some striking constellation, and tracing its progress occasionally during the night. Let him fix on one which is not too near the southern horizon, and remains a considerable time in sight, and let him view it from an east window of his house at the time of its rising, say seven o'clock in the evening, in December. He may watch it now and then till eleven o'clock, when it will have gone so much to his right that he will now find it easier to see it from the south side of the house.

He chances to awake at one o'clock, and now the constellation is *opposite* the window which looks to the south, and is higher up than the observer has previously seen it. He now closes his shutters on the calm cold stars, but, true to his undertaking, seeks his constellation again in the faint grey of the morning, shortly before seven o'clock. It is then opposite a west window, and slowly disappearing below the horizon.

Such is the progress of constellation *during one night*. We need hardly remind our readers that this apparent movement of the starry heavens is entirely caused by the real movement of the earth on its own axis.

We now proceed to trace the progress of a constellation *during a year*. Here, we have no additional *movement* to describe; the stars preserve one invariable interval between the times of their rising. All the year round they come back to their old positions in twenty-three hours, fifty-six minutes, four seconds, and one-tenth of another second; in other words, the earth takes exactly that time in making one turn on its axis.

They rise at precisely the same point of the horizon

all the year round. They mount the same height in the south, and they set at the same point of the western horizon.*

Were there no brilliant SUN in our firmament to interpose its hours of daylight, and to constrain our Earth to circle round it once a year, our observations of the stars would take the following simple form.

There would be perpetual night! and the stars *alone* would mark the periods of time. We should see them rising in uninterrupted succession; and in one cloudless interval of twenty-three hours, fifty-six minutes, four seconds, and one-tenth, the whole of the constellations would pass before our eyes, excepting those near the Southern Pole; these, as in the existing state of things, would be perpetually invisible.

But our reader, whom we have disrespectfully supposed to be familiar with no movement of the heavenly bodies, except the rising and setting of the Sun, will naturally inquire here, "Can we not in the existing state of things see all the constellations, except those near the Southern Pole, every night? And what has the Earth's annual movement round the Sun to say to the matter?"

Waiving the latter question for the present, we will answer the former by narrating the progress of a constellation during the several months of the year; hoping thereby to give an idea how any persevering

---

* The apparent or real motions of stars, enumerated in treatises on astronomy under the names of Aberration, Precession and Nutation, Proper Motion, and Parallax, are all so extremely slow as not sensibly to affect what is stated in the text.

observer can see for himself that the constellations in their turns rise in the day-time, and are for some time invisible, but that they re-appear in their appointed seasons. And to one who has watched them during even a short portion of his life, they suggest the various changes of the year almost as emphatically as the opening buds, the floral splendours, the golden harvests, and the bare and leafless forests of this earth.

We have supposed an observer watching a constellation occasionally during a winter night. If he particularly noticed the minute at which one star of that constellation rose over the horizon on December 1st, he would find that this star rose near four minutes earlier on the following evening, and on December 3rd, nearly four minutes earlier still. By New Year's Day, this star, which rose at seven o'clock on December 1st, rises two hours earlier, is plainly descending to the west at one o'clock in the morning, and sets at five instead of seven.* By February 1st it rises quite in the day-time, and consequently he cannot see it till it is already high in the sky, and it sets long before the night is over. By March 1st it is rising at one in the day-time, and at one in the morning it is setting. By June 1st it is rising at seven in the morning, and is, of course, invisible all day long. At night it is below the horizon, and, therefore, invisible also. It remains visible only in the memory of the amateur astronomer. But still observing its own invariable

* In this observation a star on the celestial equator is supposed, as it is stated, to be exactly twelve hours above the horizon. Such a star (see page 7) would rise due east of the observer.

The Observer's Apparatus.

periods, a time comes when it rises at three in the morning, namely, about the 4th of August; and should the astronomer look out for a little before the morning twilight he might see it again, soon, however, to lose it in the advancing rays of the Sun. Another month, and the star rises at one; and thus steadily gaining its two hours a month, it at length rises at the old hour of seven in the evening, shines the whole night, and is thus again in a favorable position for observation.

Some constellations are most conveniently placed in spring, others in autumn, others can scarcely be observed save in the short nights of summer. So whether he chooses it or not, the observer must learn his lesson progressively. Orion, invisible during the spring and summer, and only to be seen in autumn from "the small hours of the night" till morning, glitters in the *winter* sky as soon as the Sun has gone far enough below the horizon. Leo brightens the southern firmament in March; and the red star of Scorpio glows in the brief interval between evening and morning in the summer months.

The changes just described in the views which we obtain of the stars are entirely caused by the Earth's annual journey round the Sun. That brilliant luminary alters his position among the stars every day by a space about equal to twice his own apparent breadth. It is in reality the *Earth* which moves, making the Sun *appear* to travel between us and those stars which lie in that part of space which is in the same plane as the Earth's "orbit," or path.

We cannot, it is true, *see* this change of position. The Sun's brightness illuminates our whole atmosphere, and conceals the stars, otherwise we should see him successfully adorning " the Ram, the Bull, the heavenly Twins," and all the famous constellations of the Zodiac.

The stars surrounding the Sun, at least those which are most brilliant, have indeed been seen in the daytime during the brief interval of a total solar eclipse, and can at any time be detected by the accurately-adjusted telescopes, of an observatory. *Our* proof, however, that the Sun does thus move, or appear to move among the constellations, is, that those stars which we can see shortly after sunset, in that part of heavens opposite to the Sun, gradually diminish their distance from the region where he is placed at each successive sunset, *or rather, he approaches them*, till at the end of six months, they seem as if swallowed up in his beams, and are not visible at any part of the twenty-four hours. They are then behind the Sun, but time passes and they go on, and proceeding westward, have at length moved so far away,—or, as we have said, the Sun has so far moved from in front of them, or has *seemed* to do so in consequence of the Earth's real movement,—that they rise a little while before the Sun, and are visible again.

The maps and guides to the stars, which we have recommended, indicate the best season for observing each constellation, and commence by pointing out those northern stars which are seen all night during the whole year; proceeding next to the adjoining constellations which can scarcely be said to set, as only a few of their stars dip for a brief period below the northern horizon.

The constellations, however, which we would especially commend to the learner's attention are those which comprise the twelve signs of the Zodiac. These *signs* of the Zodiac, which divide the Sun's track into twelve equal parts, do not correspond exactly with the *constellations*, partly owing to the unequal size of the latter and partly from another reason too complicated to be treated of in this little work. Still the Sun's path lies among these stars from west to east, and were we to mark his place in a map from day to day during a year, we should find we had traced that great circle of the heavens called "the Ecliptic." This circle, instead of being everywhere equally distant from that star which marks the celestial pole, runs far to the south in our winter, and lies among stars which rise but a little way, comparatively, above the horizon, approaches daily northward till the middle of June, when it lies among stars which mount high in the sky, and remain upwards of sixteen hours above the horizon. Still sweeping round the heavens, it soon begins to recede from the north pole, and travels south, till in the following winter the circle is completed.

By learning the zodiac well we shall obtain a vivid idea of the Sun's path, and rightly apprehend the reason why he appears so low in winter, so high in summer, and why we have equal day and night in the spring and autumn. Then, we shall see why the Moon, always opposite to the Sun when full, and like the Sun always travelling in the zodiac, and rising and setting along with its neighbours for the time being, is seen towering in the sky during the long winter nights, but in summer merely skirting the southern horizon.

Lastly, by knowing the zodiac, we know where to look for the five *planets* which are visible to the naked eye. For in that region of the heavens they pursue their course, appearing, as viewed from the Earth, like bright guests in the various constellations of the zodiac, rising and setting along with them, and appearing earlier and earlier each day, till with them they disappear behind the Sun for a while.

Here, however, our well-worn book of maps is at fault. It directs us to the steady unchanging denizens of the firmament, the fixed stars, and recognises the existence of but *one* wanderer, the Sun, whose place from day to day is marked on the ecliptic. The other brilliant travellers, Mercury, Venus, Mars, Jupiter, and Saturn, must be sought in the *almanack* every year. For instance, if the reader will possess himself of 'Dietrichsen and Hannay's Almanack,' he will find the position of any of the above planets for every fifth day during the year, clearly given in " Right Ascension and Declination." He may find the map in which this spot of the heavens is contained, and just as we might mark the position of some remarkable spot on this earth, being given its longitude and latitude, he may neatly note the place of the planet among the stars, and forthwith prepare to search for and find it in the real heavens. The planet, thus identified, soon becomes a familiar acquaintance; we watch it from week to week, and in time can observe that it has its own independent movement, has changed its place in the constellation, and will at last leave it altogether. Mars, Jupiter, and Saturn are the planets most frequently in sight, while Mercury and Venus, "satellites of the Sun," as they have been termed, are seen only for a short time before the rising or after the setting of that luminary, and always in the same region of the heavens. Venus never appears further removed from the Sun than one-fourth of the celestial hemisphere; and Mercury travels away but one-sixth, and is in fact very seldom seen, as the twilight soon conceals him from view. For a few mornings before the brighter stars have paled in the sunrise, and for a few evenings after the Sun has set, he may be seen, aptly realizing the title, "messenger of the gods," by his rapid movement. Venus is much longer in sight, occasionally remaining visible four hours after sunset, or preceding the rising of the Sun by that interval.

But Mars, Jupiter, and Saturn can be seen in quite the opposite quarter of the heavens from the Sun, and are frequently visible during the whole night. Thus we can easily trace their paths, and note them from month to month, and year to year. These planets seem to move, like the Sun, round the zodiac from west to east through the main part of their journey, yet sometimes they appear to stand still for a few days, then they actually go backward a little way, and then again they stand, then once more move eastward. The eastward movement is real, their own steady course round the Sun, but the little backward run and the two pauses, are the result of our Earth's motion in her smaller path round the Sun making them appear to run in the opposite direction when in a particular position. Mercury and Venus also perform this little piece of retrograde movement, but as the neighbouring stars are not so often visible with them, as in the case of the three outer planets, it cannot be so easily watched.

Very slowly and solemnly does the planet Saturn make its way round the Sun. When we first noted its position it was in the constellation Pisces, and two stars in Aries pointed downwards to it. That was in the spring of 1850; and thirty years from that period must elapse before the eye of man will see it there again. Since then it has passed through Aries and Taurus, and is now east of the principal stars in Gemini. Jupiter, taking only twelve years to travel round the Sun, has passed over eight of the constellations of the zodiac in the same period. Mars performs its circuit in a little more than two years, as viewed from the Earth.

If the observer wishes to obtain a clear idea of the path of a planet, he cannot do better than note its successive places on his map by means of the almanacks for two or three years. Then drawing a line from point to point, he will observe that it is very similar to the Ecliptic, but at certain intervals there will occur a little loop or *double*, where the planet has stood still, gone back, and after a pause resumed its grand eastward progress. The path of the Moon is free from these interruptions. Its apparent rapidity, too, is greater, almost beyond comparison, as it encircles the

The Observer's Apparatus.

zodiac in a month. It moves farther north, and also farther south than the Sun, but follows the same direction, namely, from east to west.

To give an idea how to use the almanack as a guide to the planets, we may mention as an example, their position on January 21st, 1857. On that evening, and also for a few evenings before and after it, all the five planets known to the ancients were visible for a short interval after sunset, a fact which we ascertained by conning page 6 of 'Dietrichsen and Hannay's Almanack' for a few minutes. The lower part of this page was devoted to a table of the rising, southing, and setting of the planets, calculated for every fifth day during the month. It appeared that four of them set in the evening, as follows:—Mercury at 6h. 6m.; Mars at 7h. 37m.; Venus at 8h. 30m.; Jupiter at 10h. 23m. On the same evening the Sun, according to a column in another part of the page, was to set at 4h. 27m., so that this gave an interval of one hour and thirty-nine minutes in which Mercury might be seen; the three others being longer in sight.

The next question was, Can Saturn possibly be also visible? Yes, he will be quite high enough above the horizon, for he rose at 2h. 25m. in the afternoon. Referring now to the short columns at the top of the page, we find the "right ascensions" of the five planets for this day; that is to say, their places answering to what we should call east Longitude* on the terrestrial

---

* Longitude on the terrestrial globe is reckoned east and west of the "first meridian."

Right ascension is reckoned east only, and the reckoning begins

globe: they are as follows:—Mercury 21h. 20m. 26s.; Mars 22h. 22m. 53s.; Venus 23h. 4m. 59s.; Jupiter 0h. 18m. 50s.; Saturn 6h. 39m. 40s. "0," be it observed, is marked 24 on the map, and means the same thing, therefore the four first-mentioned planets are apparently near each other; we find the numbers corresponding to the above all in the same map, but Saturn is far off, half way to the opposite part of the heavens. Next we found their *declination,* which answers to *Latitude** on the terrestrial globe. It is given at the top of page 7 of the almanack, thus:— Mercury 14h. 21m. 35s., south; Mars 10h. 27m. 12s., south; Venus 6h. 54m. 1s., south; Jupiter 0h. 42m.

from a line running through the first point of the *sign* Aries, which, however, is about the centre of the constellation Pisces.

Right ascension is marked in *hours*, and sometimes in *degrees* also. There are fifteen degrees to an hour. In 'Middleton's Atlas' both divisions are given. In 'Dietrichsen and Hannay's Almanack,' hours, minutes, and seconds only are given; and in 'Gall's Atlas,' degrees only. We recommend the student to mark the hours also on the margin of these maps.

* Latitude on the terrestrial globe is reckoned north and south of the equator.

Declination is reckoned north and south also, and the reckoning is from the celestial equator, that great imaginary circle which is everywhere equally distant from the poles of the heavens.

In 'Dietrichsen and Hannay's Almanack,' and in 'Middleton's Atlas,' the places of the stars are given in declination; but in some other almanacks, and in 'Gall's Atlas,' they are given in north polar distance, by which measure the stars on the celestial equator would be marked as in ninety degrees of north polar distance, those ten degrees south declination as in one hundred degrees, and so on.

We recommend the student to mark the numbers in declination at every tenth degree, on the margin of Gall's maps, and with a hard pencil to rule lines across the map from each of these, and similar ones from the hours of right ascension.

59s., north; Saturn 22h. 37m. 6s., north. We now marked the exact points on the maps, and also noted the Sun's place on the ecliptic; and clearly proved to ourselves that the four neighbouring planets would be arranged nearly in a line, slanting upward, Jupiter being the most distant from the Sun, and Mercury nearest to him. It was a fine evening, and from no better observatory than a railway carriage, we watched the Sun descending below the horizon, and, allowing for the sloping course he was still pursuing, though concealed from our eyes, knew where to expect Jupiter and Venus to appear in the increasing darkness. There they were; and as star by star shone out in the blue concave, our eyes suddenly detected Mars a little way to the west of Venus, and then Mercury, gleaming brightly close to the last rays of the Sun. We next sought out Saturn, and a glance from the east window of the carriage showed him, ornamenting the constellation of Gemini.

This reminiscence of January, 1857, may sufficiently serve as a hint how to use the almanack. It only remains now to point out, in a general way, some of the more interesting subjects for observation with a small TELESCOPE.

We will do so in the form of a list, premising that nearly all the phenomena noted here are predicted in the almanack.

The constantly changing positions of Jupiter's satellites.

The apparent widening and narrowing of Saturn's ring during fifteen years.

The phases of Mercury and Venus, and of Mars, the two former of which frequently appear crescent-shaped, and the latter gibbous, or not quite circular.

The variety in the apparent diameters of the planets depending on their distance from the Earth. The diameter of Venus appears nearly six times more at some periods than at others. The apparent size of Jupiter varies in a much less degree, the difference being in the proportion of about three to four and a half.

Eclipses of the Sun and Moon.

Occultations of the stars, and occasionally of planets, by the Moon passing in front of them; for instance, the Moon concealed Jupiter for more than an hour on January 2nd, 1857, and the planet's re-appearance formed a beautiful spectacle through the telescope.

Conjunctions of any of the planets; that is to say, the apparent meeting or near approach of any two or more of them, are at all times striking and beautiful, and enable observers to compare them, and to trace their subsequent wanderings with renewed interest.

Of Astronomical phenomena, not noted in the almanack, but particularly suited for observation with the telescope, we may name the following :—

The spots on the Sun, showing the rotation of that luminary on its axis in twenty-five days.

The craters and elevations of the Moon, with their sharply-defined shadows, moving as the Sun's light gradually shines on them.

The irregular belts of Jupiter, showing his rotation on his axis.

Some objects among the fixed stars are also seen more clearly with a small telescope than with the unassisted eye; namely, a few clusters of stars, the great nebular in Orion, and some of the more conspicuous double stars.

Finally, the observer may chance to find a *Comet*, not with his telescope, in the starry heavens, but humbly *in the newspaper,* and studying the printed tables, mark its place on the map for several successive days, and then watch for it in the same manner as if it were a planet.

We will now conduct our reader to those heavenly bodies which we have observed from year to year, and at the same time endeavour to impart some of the discoveries of the learned in connection with each.

CHAPTER II.

THE SUN.

LET us place at the beginning of our observations this magnificent orb. It is, of all the heavenly bodies, the one most frequently in our thoughts. It is the brightest thing which the Lord of Glory has been pleased to show us in this life. It is the source of light and heat to our earth.

First let us describe its appearance as seen through our little instrument, and then proceed to narrate some of the discoveries which, by means of the telescope, have hitherto been made concerning this stupendous globe.

We must place a piece of dark-coloured glass before the eye-piece of the telescope, as the Sun is far too bright to be looked at without this protection. There are two other little precautions which we would recommend to the observer; firstly, to point the telescope by observing its shadow on a piece of paper, held to receive it; when this shadow is perfectly round, it will be found that the instrument is exactly pointing to the Sun; secondly, prepare a flat piece of pasteboard, with a hole cut through it of the diameter of the telescope, and when the instrument is properly adjusted, slip on the pasteboard to screen the unemployed eye and the head and

PARTIAL ECLIPSE OF MOON.

THE MOON,
Two days and twenty-one hours after New.

THE SUN, on *March 18th*, 1858, *shewing a remarkable spot on its surface.*

Sun, as seen with the naked eye, through smoked glass.

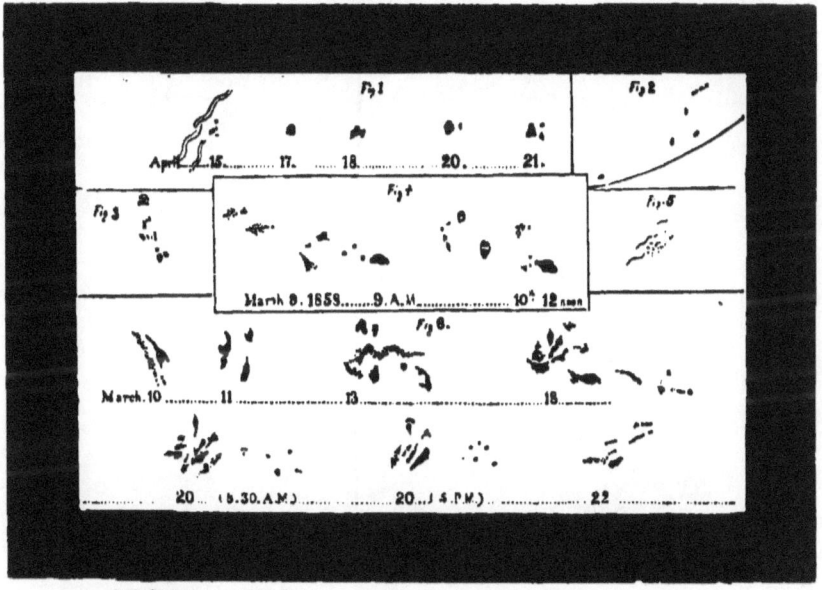

SOLAR SPOTS, OBSERVED AT VARIOUS TIMES.

Fig. 1. Spot, observed April 15 to 21, 1854.   Fig. 2. Spot, close to the Sun's edge, April 12, 1854.
Fig. 3 Spot, May 11, 1854.   Fig. 4. Spot, observed on two successive days.
Fig. 5 Luminous marks on the Sun, March 10, 1858.   Fig. 6. Spot, March 10 to 22, 1858.

face from the heat of the Sun. The first precaution is recommended to save the observer from being dazzled in vain endeavours to "hit the Sun" in the ordinary way, and both are more easily and quickly done in practice than in description.

Looking now through the telescope, should the dark glass used be of a reddish shade, we shall see a round orange-coloured disc in a black sky. On this disc there are generally a few black spots, somewhat resembling small blots or splashes of ink. When examined with care the larger spots prove to be not uniformly black, and not circular in shape, but of two dark shades, and of irregular outline. It is somewhat practicable to look at the sun through a fog or thin cloud without using the coloured glass. Its disc then appears white, and the spots are of two shades of brown.

The opinion generally held by astronomers concerning these spots is, that they are the *comparatively dark solid body of the Sun*, laid bare to our view by immense fluctuations in its luminous atmosphere ;* that the Sun has at least two atmospheres, upper and lower, and that the *darker* part of the spots is where the sun is seen through a rent in *both* layers of atmosphere ; the *lighter*, where one layer still covers it.* Recent observations have indicated that there are *three* gradations of shade, in some spots at least, the centre being the darkest.†

The solar spots are not permanent. When watched from day to day, they are observed to enlarge or contract, to change their forms, and at length to disappear

* Herschel's 'Treatise,' p. 208-9.
† Johnston's 'School Atlas of Astronomy,' p. 4.

altogether; and new ones appear where previously there were none. These changes can be detected with a very small telescope. Another phenomenon on the Sun's disc is the occasional appearance of certain branching streaks of light on its luminous surface, curved in shape, and distinguished by their superior brightness. These are called *faculæ*, and are often observed in the neighbourhood of great spots, or on parts of the solar disc, where spots shortly afterwards break out. These have been supposed to be the ridges of immense waves in the luminous regions of the Sun's atmosphere, indicative of violent agitation in their vicinity.*

With powerful instruments the whole surface of the Sun may be seen to be finely mottled with minute dark dots or pores, which fluctuate in their appearance like the rest of the markings.*

The solar disc can be exhibited in a very agreeable manner by holding a screen or sheet of paper at a proper distance from the eye-piece of the telescope, and slightly altering the focus of the instrument, when the bright image of the Sun will be shown, with all the spots distinctly appearing. The effect will be heightened by darkening the room, as, for instance, by having a hole made in the window-shutter for the telescope, and closing every other aperture. The *faculæ* show particularly well in this way, and their presence may often be thus detected when the fatigued eye has failed to observe them by a direct scrutiny. With this contrivance, however, the spots will be reversed, as in a camera obscura; but they may be noted down on

* Herschel's 'Treatise,' p. 208.

paper, and afterwards traced on the other side, when they will appear in their true positions.

The changes in these spots are truly surprising when we consider the size of the Sun; and its size is known with considerable exactness, having been calculated by comparing its apparent diameter by its known distance.*

And how is the Sun's distance known? It is no doubt difficult to conceive the way in which the distance of *any* inaccessible point can be ascertained. Surveyors use an instrument by which they can tell *the direction* of any far-off tree or building, *as seen from each end of a line, which they have actually measured on the ground*, and knowing the two directions, and the length of the " base line," they can by arithmetical calculations tell the *distance* of a tree or building;† and it is by a nearly similar process, on a far larger scale, and performed with excellent instruments, that the distances of the Sun and planets have been computed. The *base line*, answering to the surveyor's line measured on the ground, has been as long as from Britain to the Cape of Good Hope, or from Lapland to Otaheite.‡

And the Sun is so far off that its light takes more than eight minutes to reach the Earth,§ and yet light requires *but one second* to travel one hundred and ninety-two thousand miles. ||

* Herschel's 'Treatise,' p. 192.
† Ibid., p. 147, and see chap. xii of this little book.
‡ Airy's 'Lectures on Astronomy,' p. 139.
§ 'Cosmos,' vol. iii, p. 269.
|| Herschel's 'Treatise.' p. 297.

It must then be of stupendous size to appear so large as it does at such a distance. Some spots have frequently appeared on it large enough to be visible to the naked eye.* One of these was forty-five thousand miles in diameter, three times as long as the voyage from England to Australia! "That such a spot should close up in six weeks' time (for they hardly ever last longer) its borders must approach at the rate of more than a thousand miles a day." †

The solar spots were discovered by Galileo in 1610.‡ It was soon observed that besides changing their shapes in the way above described, they always approached the Sun's edge with a motion of the same kind as that which an island on a globe would seem to have, if we fixed our eyes on it, while we slowly turned the globe.

This movement proves that the Sun revolves on its axis, a fact which could not otherwise have been easily ascertained.§ A spot of great size, and for some days visible to the naked eye is shown in Plate II, fig. 2. The course of these spots varies with the period of the year at which they are observed. From this fact astronomers have discovered that the Sun's axis is not perpendicular to the Earth's annual orbit. In September the Sun's north pole is most turned towards us; in March its south pole is similarly situated, and the spots pursue a curved course, corresponding with these positions; whereas in June and December they appear

---

* 'Cosmos,' vol. iii, p. 275.
† Herschel's 'Treatise,' p. 208.
‡ 'Martyrs of Science,' p. 36.
§ Arago's 'Lectures on Astronomy,' p. 18.

to traverse the disc in straight lines.* The time of the Sun's rotation on its axis is twenty-five days and eight hours.*

It is a remarkable circumstance that the solar spots always occur near the Sun's equator, where his rotation must be quickest; a region corresponding to the tropics of this Earth, where the fiercest whirlwinds and hurricanes of our atmosphere occur.†

We have now described at some length the Sun's thinly-scattered *spots*, but what shall we say of its *brightness*, its radiant beams, which return to our eyes in such splendour even when reflected from the far-distant orb of Saturn? What of its genial life-dispensing heat?

"The question, 'Whence are thy beams, O Sun?' remains as unanswered now as in the days of Ossian, and the manner in which this perpetual light and heat are kept undimmed, is as great a mystery as life itself."‡ A mystery to us, but no mystery to "the Father of Lights," who " maketh his Sun to rise on the evil and on the good."

* Johnston's 'School Atlas.'
† Nichol's 'Cyclopædia of Physical Science,' p. 710.
‡ Breen's 'Planetary Worlds,' p. 39.

CHAPTER III.

THE EARTH.

DOES our reader complain that we have already departed from the province of this little book, as stated in our introduction?

We have promised to treat only of those heavenly bodies which we can observe, and are we not already following in the track of the school-books, and placing old mother Earth among the heavenly bodies for mere custom's sake?

Reader, we cannot, it is true, direct our little telescope so as to gain a bird's-eye view of this world. Neither we, nor any of the human race, can at any one time behold more than an insignificant portion of its surface.

In this matter, as well as in that of self-knowledge how difficult it is

"To see ourselves as others see us!"

Yet, though we cannot see the Earth, we can now and then see in the moon-lit heavens its silhouette, a portion of its round black portrait, clearly suspended before our eyes; and again at another time, the reflection of its *brightness* though not of its form comes to our eyes, "as in a mirror, darkly." Thus we may place it among *observed* phenomena, as in a collection of portraits from life, we might admit the silhouette and the shadowy photograph, rather than altogether exclude one whose likeness is not to be had in any form.

The Earth exhibits its *black portrait* at the time of a lunar eclipse. That dark shade with a curved edge, which glides on those occasions over the Moon's bright disc, is no other than the shadow of this round world, (Plate 1, fig. 1). It would be exhibited at every full moon, but that on account of the Moon's moving in a path which is not exactly in the same plane with that of the Earth, it but seldom happens that Earth, Moon, and Sun, are in a straight line.

To the observer who is favoured with a clear sky on the occasion of an eclipse of the Moon, it is a striking and suggestive sight. The accuracy with which it commences at its predicted time, and the distinctly-rounded form of the shadow, produce a strong feeling of the *truth* of Astronomy.

The other sight in the heavens, which tells us not of the Earth's form, but of its brightness, is that lovely spectacle, popularly called "the old moon in the young moon's arms." Shortly before and shortly after new Moon, when the illuminated portion of our satellite seems only like a narrow bow, a pale ashy light plays on the remainder of the disc, rendering it faintly visible, (Plate I, fig. 2). That is Earthlight on the Moon, "the reflection of a reflection." For then the Earth is (so to speak) nearly *full* of the Moon, and its light reflected from the Sun, shines on the Moon, and that with sufficient brilliancy to make it visible to us after a second reflection.

With these two phenomena before our eyes, we see, and we feel anew, constrained to believe that this Earth is indeed no level plain, but a globe, and that it shines like Venus, Mars, and the other planetary worlds. And yet it seems strange, as we look at the solid substance of this Earth, that it could under any circumstances appear like a Star! But as Sir John Herschel remarks in stating that the Moon's light is entirely derived from reflection, it need not be thought surprising " that a solid substance should appear to shine." " It is no more than a white cloud does standing off upon the clear blue sky. By day the Moon can hardly be distinguished in brightness from such a cloud; and in the dusk of evening clouds catching the last rays of the Sun appear with a dazzling splendour, not inferior to the seeming brightness of the moon at night." Thus we may conceive how the Earth illuminated by sunshine may be seen from far, gleaming like the Moon or a planet.

The first European records of astronomy are those of Alonzo the Tenth, King of Castile, A.D. 1250. He was the greatest patron of astronomy in his age, and it is related that he objected to the complicated system devised by Ptolemy.

It remained for Copernicus, a Danish astronomer, nearly to unfold the true theory of the planets. He applied himself to astronomy in 1500, but his work, the name of which was "On the Revolutions of the

The Earth.

Heavenly Bodies," was not published till 1543. He died that very year. Three years afterwards was born the illustrious Tycho Brahe, who at the age of fourteen began to study astronomy, and was the best observer since Hipparchus. His observations guided Kepler in the discovery of the famous "laws" of astronomy which bear his name. Contemporary with Kepler was Galileo, who made a *Telescope* in 1609; and who was the first to answer certain serious objections to the theory of Copernicus. From this time down to the present day we meet with numerous illustrious names in the annals of astronomy, and pre-eminent among them all is that of NEWTON. Others had laboured at the edifice of Truth, contributing to its perfection from age to age, but as it were in darkness, waiting for the dawn of light. He first dispersed the shades of night, and shed on the beauteous structure the bright beams of intellect, placing it in perpetual sunshine.

No reader of this little work will require to be informed that Newton's great discovery was that of Universal Gravitation. It may, however, be well to state *what* was the distinctive feature of this discovery, as peculiarly belonging to Newton.

It was this; that he demonstrated, by studying the motions and distances of the Sun, Moon, and planets, that this grand, all-pervading force of attraction, exercised by each particle of matter on every other particle, is an absolute fact, a great law of nature, and not a mere theory suggested without proof as a way of accounting for observed phenomena.*

* 'Penny Cyclopædia,' article "Astronomy."

In 1666 Newton began particularly to reflect on the force which makes bodies fall to the surface of the Earth, and to conjecture that the same force might even influence the far-off Moon. It is possible, thought he, that the Earth attracts the Moon, and that this in connexion with an original "projectile" force, is what causes it to move in the curved path, and with the variable velocity which have been observed. The next question was, "Does the Moon advance towards the Earth in the exact proportion in which it ought to advance, if it be indeed influenced by the same force which draws a stone or an apple to the ground?" He compared the measures of the Moon's distance and the Earth's diameter, according to the computations which had been made at that period; and it appeared to him that the force of the Earth's attraction would *not* be sufficient to account for the observed motion of the Moon. He had therefore not found the proof he sought; and his biographers relate that for sixteen years he discarded the theory of universal gravitation.*

But in 1682 he heard the particulars of a more correct measurement of the Earth than that from which he had previously calculated. He resumed his investigations, and found that his former ideas were based on truth. He followed out the subject in its various bearings, established unerring rules for calculating the effects of gravitation, and proved, in successive sections of his great work, the 'Principia,' that

---

* 'Penny Cyclopædia,' article "Newton."

these rules hold good alike for objects on the Earth, and for the Moon, planets, and comets.*

Succeeding mathematicians have applied these rules to the minutest details of the most intricate planetary motions; and, to quote Professor Airy's works, when we "compare the observed place of a planet with the place which was calculated beforehand, according to the law of gravitation, it is found that they agree so nearly as to leave no doubt of the truth of the law. The motion of Jupiter, for instance, is so perfectly calculated, that astronomers have computed ten years beforehand the time at which it will pass the meridian of different places, [that is to say the instant at which we, for instance, should see it exactly opposite a south window,] and we find the predicted moment correct within half a second of time."†

We will not now enter into these achievements of science further than to give *three simple proofs of the globular*‡ *form of the Earth*, and to allude in a few words to the beautiful arrangement which causes the change of seasons.

Firstly, the sharp horizon line at sea, not fading away in the distance, as would be the case if the sea extended over a level plain, but forming round our station a circle, behind which receding vessels disappear, just as if they descended below the brow of a hill.

Secondly, the fact that as we travel long distances to the south, stars which as seen from the British Isles

---

* 'Penny Cyclopædia,' article "Principia."

† Ibid., article "Gravitation."

‡ More correctly speaking "spheroidal," the earth being slightly flattened at its poles.

merely skirted the southern horizon, appear high in the heavens, and new stars, never before beheld by us, come into view.

Still further south these newly seen constellations shine directly overhead, and those surrounding the northern pole have disappeared from our view. Again, as we travel northward of the British Isles the northern stars rise higher than we have hitherto seen them, and always in exact proportion to the latitude from which they are observed.

Thirdly, people have sailed round the Earth. Magellan first accomplished this feat; it was next done by Sir Francis Drake, and every one has heard of the voyage of Captain Cook. Ships are now "almost daily prosecuting such voyages. It is a common thing for ships to sail in an easterly direction to Australia, and to return by continuing their eastward course, and not by coming back the same way they set out."*

This last forms the strongest practical proof of all, and gained by direct experiment and observation, that *our world is round.*

The diameter of the Earth is nearly eight thousand miles. Any inequalities on its surface must therefore bear a very minute proportion to the whole size of the planet. "The highest mountain does not exceed five miles in perpendicular elevation; this is only one sixteen hundredth part of the Earth's diameter; consequently on a globe of sixteen inches in diameter, such a mountain would be represented by a protuberance of no more than one hundredth part of an inch, which is

* Airy's 'Lectures.'

The Earth.

about the thickness of ordinary drawing-paper."* On the same scale fine sand or dust would represent smaller mountains, scratches and pin-holes imperceptible without a magnifier would suffice for the deepest mines, the depths of the sea would be imitated by a slight depression in about the same proportion as the height of the mountains, and a mere film of liquid would represent the ocean.

The subject of the seasons is clearly explained in every elementary book on astronomy, and proved to be a result of the oblique position of the Earth's axis. Had it been placed perpendicular to the plane of the Earth's path round the Sun, the following would have been the effect:—There would have been equal day and night all over the globe, and at all times of year. By its being on the contrary, obliquely placed, the northern parts of the Earth have long days and short nights in summer; the Sun at noon is high in the heavens, and throughout his daily course is the companion of those stars which set but for a short time (see page 13;) and the polar regions have for some weeks no night at all. In the southern latitudes they have short days and long nights at the time it is summer to the northern hemisphere. Six months afterwards, when there is winter in the north, there is summer south of the Equator, and at the intermediate periods of spring and autumn, there is equal day and night all over the world.

We now once more take leave of our planet, and turn our attention to our nearest neighbour in space.

* Herschel's 'Treatise,' p. 22.

CHAPTER IV.

THE MOON.

THIS is the nearest of all the heavenly bodies. Its frequent changes of position and shape must attract every one's attention; both are the effect of its moving round the earth once in four weeks. The inequalities on its surface visible to the naked eye, become more and more interesting as we view them with more and more powerful telescopes.

At the time of full Moon, when the Sun's light illuminates the whole lunar disc which is opposite to us, we of course see the greatest possible part of its surface, but we do not by any means see it to the best advantage. It is like viewing a large building with the light shining strongly in front of it, and making it appear without any shadows.

It would be more picturesquely shown with the sunshine coming from one side, and bringing out the different projections in light and shade.

Accordingly the most favorable time for observing it is during eight or nine days before, and a similar period after new Moon.

The Moon turns on its axis in exactly the time which it occupies in revolving round the Earth; thus

it keeps the same side continually directed towards us.*
There are *slight* variations called "librations," in the
direction in which we see the Moon; a little more of
its western side is brought into view at one time than
at another, while a small portion of the eastern side is
concealed, and *vice versâ;* also, owing to the fact that
the Moon's axis is not quite perpendicular to the plane
of her path round the earth, the Moon's north and
south poles incline slightly towards the earth in their
turns; so that we are acquainted with the appearance
of a little more than one hemisphere.† But the remaining part is to us an impenetrable mystery.

However, of the visible part of the Moon we can
make a better map than of that "half of the Earth's
surface which comprises the interior of Asia and
Africa."‡ In fact such a map exists; we allude to the
large chart of the Moon, published by Beer and Mädler,
in 1834; a work of exquisite accuracy, "containing
every winding of every bay, every rocky promontory,
every steep defile, every mountain and vale, every
hollow, plain, and river, if such a thing exists, until
there is not a peculiar feature of her scenery" that is
not recorded for our inspection.§

Of all the heavenly bodies, the Moon is beyond
comparison that of whose physical constitution we can

* Herschel's 'Treatise,' p. 230. † Ibid., p. 231.
‡ 'Cosmos,' vol. iii, p. 359.
§ This quotation is from Rev. J. Crampton's book, 'The Lunar World,' a highly interesting work, in which a very successful attempt is made to realize lunar landscape and scenery; and an instructive detail given of the many beneficent arrangements in connection with our satellite.

learn most. With the aid of even a small telescope, its highly diversified surface presents a strange and striking appearance, and one to which the observer must devote some time and study, before he can become even moderately familiar with its details. Riccioli, a distinguished *savant* of the seventeenth century, performed a piece of good service to the students of the Moon, by giving names to the various parts of its surface.* He styled the broad-shaded tracts seas, oceans, etc.; for instance, there is the Sea of Serenity, the Sea of Showers, the Ocean of Storms. He called the mountains after the most celebrated astronomers of ancient and modern times; and a few bear the names of well-known mountains in the Earth.* The observer soon becomes well acquainted with the conspicuous and brilliant summits of Tycho, Copernicus, Kepler, and Aristarchus; the strangely dark "craters" of Plato and Grimaldus, and the glittering ridge of the Lunar Appenines. (Plate III.)

The lunar mountains are wonderfully numerous, occupying by far the larger portion of the surface. They are almost all of a circular or cup-shaped form. The larger ones have for the most part small, steep, conical hills rising up in their craters. " They offer, in short, in its highest perfection," says Sir John Herschel, "the true *volcanic* character, as it may be seen in the crater of Vesuvius, and in a map of the Campi Phlegrai or the Puy de Dome."†

Herschel adds from his own observations, that decisive

* 'Penny Cyclopædia,' article " Moon."
† Herschel's 'Treatise,' p. 229.

marks of volcanic stratification, arising from successive deposits of ejected matter, may be clearly traced with powerful telescopes.

It must, however, be remembered, that the craters of the Moon are of vastly larger dimensions than those of the Earth. For instance, a remarkable lunar crater called Tycho, is nearly fifty miles in diameter;* and this is by no means one of the widest. A few spots on the Moon shine with a peculiar brightness, which it has been suggested may be caused by some mirror-like concentration of rays. One of these, a crater called Aristarchus, is believed to be the same spot at which Sir William Herschel saw what he supposed to be a burning volcano. But Mr. Nasmyth, of Manchester, who has spent all the leisure of many years in examining the Moon with powerful telescopes, and who has seen the effects of volcanic action in different parts of the Earth, is decidedly of opinion that not one of the numerous volcanos on the lunar surface is in action, or has been so for thousands of years past.†

These hollow mountains prevail on almost all parts of the Moon's surface; there are, however, some chains of mountains with exceedingly pointed summits.‡ When such summits appear near the shaded part of the Moon, that is, on the inner edge of the crescent, they shine like detached points on stars. This appearance never fails to surprise an observer who looks for the first time at the Moon through a telescope.

* Nichol's 'Cyclopædia,' p. 515.
† 'The Lunar World,' p. 99.
‡ 'Cosmos,' vol. iii, p. 353.

(Plate I, fig. 2, and plate IV, figs. 5, 6.) The inner edge of the Moon seems like melting ice, with bright drops hanging from it. These *drops* are in fact the mountain tops on which the Sun has risen, while the valleys remain in shade.

The height of the lunar mountains has been calculated by observations made on the length of their shadows. The higher the mountain the longer the shadow.* It is interesting to observe the *foreshortening* of the mountains and valleys; those opposite our eyes appearing *round*, and those near the Moon's edge *elliptical*.†

The lunar mountains are very high. Thirty-eight of them are higher than Mont Blanc; ‡ none, however, equal in height the loftiest summit of the Himalaya.§ But these mountains are very lofty *in proportion to the Moon's size;* its diameter being two thousand one hundred and sixty miles,‖ whereas that of the Earth is nearly eight thousand miles.

It has been asked "why does the outer edge of the Moon appear so smooth, instead of bristling all round with these lofty mountains?" To this we answer, that high as these mountains are, they still bear a very small *absolute* proportion to the dimensions of the Moon. Let the reader glance at our scale of English miles in Plate III, which, however, is chiefly applicable

---

* Arago's 'Lectures,' p. 21.
† Herschel's 'Treatise,' p. 229.
‡ 'Cosmos,' vol. iii, p. 363.
§ Ibid., p. 131.
‖ Herschel's 'Treatise,' p. 214.

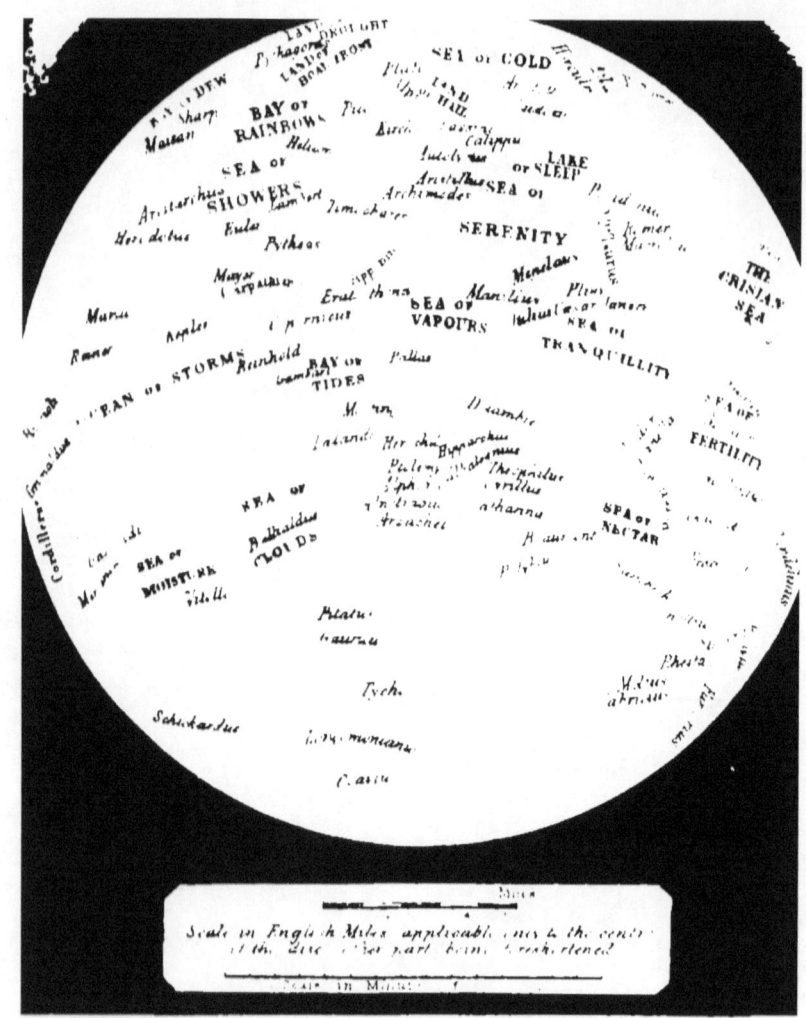

MAP OF THE MOON
with the names given by Riccioli in the 18th century
and others added by succeeding observers

to the centre of the lunar map, on account of the remainder of the disc being more or less fore-shortened. The highest lunar mountain rises to about four miles and a half. On our map, therefore, that would be represented by an excrescence of about the twenty-second part of one of the divisions of one hundred miles on the scale; and its visibility would be lessened by other mountains rising around it, and partly concealing its sides. It is, however, true that with powerful instruments the profiles of the lunar mountains can, under favorable circumstances, be occasionally seen, especially when at the time of a solar eclipse, the Moon is "held, as it were, to the candle of our system."* On such occasions its mountains have been observed intensely black, in relief against the Sun's disc.

There is one singular feature of lunar scenery which we will now describe. At the time of full Moon, and for some days before and after that period, when the lunar mountains and valleys, as we have already remarked, are *least* visible from being deprived of their shadows, certain narrow streaks of light may be observed radiating from some of the craters. They are not lines of mountains, they do not cast any shadows, and they run in an undeviating course, and with undiminished brightness, to vast distances across the surface of the planet. The most extensive of these radiating systems is that which proceeds from Tycho, and in which more than a hundred streaks of light can be distinguished. The mountains of Kepler, Copernicus,

* Rev. J. Crampton.

and Aristarchus, are also surrounded by these mysterious rays, which appear as silent witnesses of the devastating activity of the lunar volcanos in times long past. It can plainly be seen that they have been formed at different periods; rays from Kepler, for instance, cutting through and slightly effacing rays from Copernicus and Aristarchus, while rays from Aristarchus also cut through rays from Copernicus.* Copernicus is therefore the oldest of these three radiating craters. Tycho is believed to be the earliest of all.*

Mr. Nasmyth tried the experiment of cracking by expansion glass globes filled perfectly full of water, and hermetically sealed, and the rays produced bore a striking resemblance to those from the lunar craters. He believes the streaks on the Moon to have been similarly produced by underground forces, which cracked the lunar crust, and this fracture was, he supposes, followed by an "exudation of very fluid lava up through the cracks, simultaneously along their entire course, in the same way as water would come up through cracks in the ice resting on the surface of water below." Mr. Nasmyth considers that the molten matter would "spread somewhat at the surface, so that a crack of twenty feet wide might yield a streak of a mile wide or so, according to the fluidity of the lava." He believes these rays, and the brilliancy of some of the lunar craters, to be the most recent of the Moon's features.

Mr. Nasmyth's ideas on this subject are received

---

* Professor Nichol, quoted in the 'Lunar World.'

as standard ones by the highest astronomical authorities.*

The Moon has no clouds, or any other indication of an atmosphere.† Wide and apparently level tracts in the Moon have, as we have already related, received the name of *seas*. When examined, however, with powerful telescopes, they exhibit sundry inequalities, and other appearances which lead astronomers to consider them not seas but tracts of low land.† It is indeed not believed that there is any water in the Moon.

Without air or water, if such *be* the Moon's condition, it seems impossible that it can sustain inhabitants formed like ourselves.‡ If there are inhabitants of any kind capable of *seeing*, the Earth must present to them a curious spectacle. It must appear almost four times as broad as the Moon does to us, and exhibiting the same phases; that is, sometimes round, sometimes semicircular, sometimes crescent shaped.

When at the full they might possibly trace the various continents and oceans on its surface. Their outlines, however, would generally be made indistinct by intervening clouds in the Earth's atmosphere.§

This spectacle would of course be presented to the inhabitants of only *one* side of the Moon; they would observe the Earth turning daily on its axis, but almost immoveably fixed in their sky, always the same height

---

* 'Lunar World,' p. 9.
† Herschel's 'Treatise,' p. 229.
‡ Ibid., p. 230.
§ 'Cosmos,' vol. iii, p. 130.

above their horizon, or, rather very nearly so, as the Moon's "librations," (see page 37,) would cause the position of the Earth in the Moon's sky to vary in a slight degree.

A curious effect of the absence of air would be that this brilliant globe, the Earth, would appear against a sky *almost black.**

Though the Earth never sets to the Moon, that is to the one side which we see of the Moon, the *Sun* does so.† It successively illuminates all portions of the Moon's surface, during the Moon's monthly rotation on its axis. Taking into consideration the fact that the Moon has no clouds to moderate the heat it receives from the Sun, Sir John Herschel concludes that its climate must be very extraordinary; the alternation being that of unmitigated and burning sunshine, fiercer than an equatorial noon, continued for a whole fortnight, and the keenest severity of frost, far exceeding that of our polar winters, for an equal time.‡ The Moon's day and night are in fact also its summer and winter.

Observations of the Moon's place in the heavens, are highly advantageous to voyagers, as a means of *finding the longitude*; that is, the distance of the observer to the east or west of the first meridian.§ Let us endeavour to give some idea of this method of finding longitudes. The *desideratum* in a calculation of longi-

---

* 'Cosmos,' vol. iii, p. 358.
† Herschel's 'Treatise.' p. 228.   ‡ Ibid., p. 230.
§ This explanation of lunar observations is abridged from Herschel's 'Treatise,' p. 143—146.

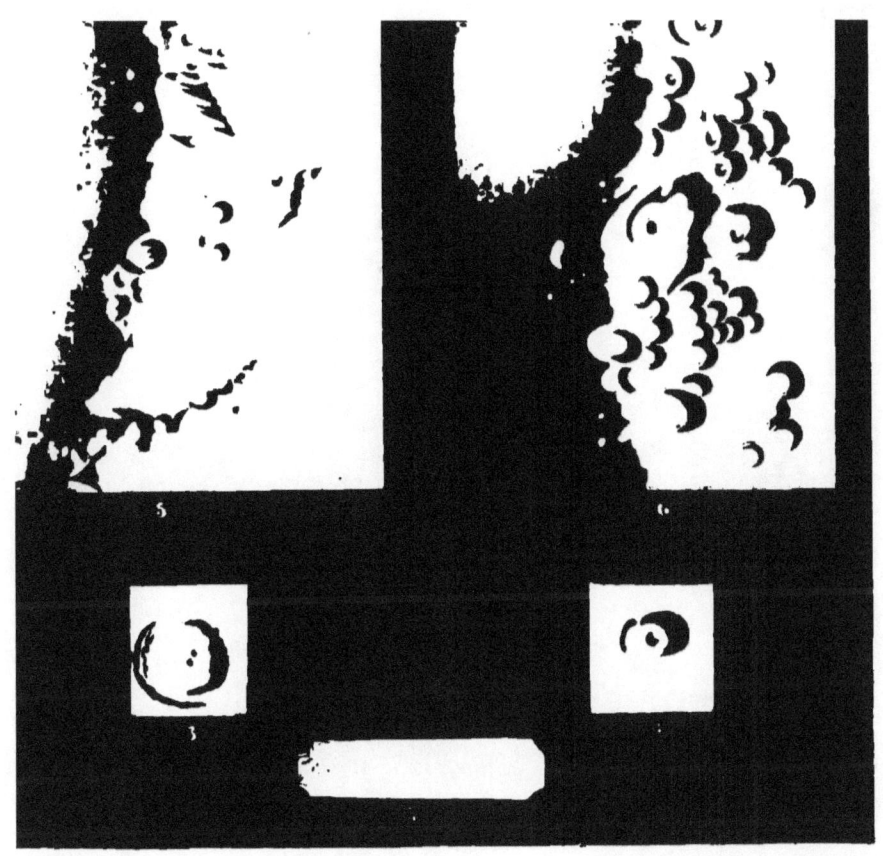

tude is this, to ascertain what o'clock it is at the first meridian, in other words, according to the reckoning of the British nation, "what o'clock it is at *Greenwich*," at the moment when the calculation is made. For the hour of the day is not alike all over the world. The Sun will have reached "its highest noon" in England while it is only early morning to the inhabitants of America; and at that very hour of noon in England, the dwellers in far eastern countries are enjoying the coolness of evening. The greater the difference in longitude, the greater will be the difference of time.

The hour of the day at any part of the world is ascertained by noting the moment at which the Sun is at its highest point. At that time it is noon by the Sun. A seaman duly practised in taking such observations, can thus readily discover his "local time."* And if he could possibly tell what o'clock it then was at Greenwich, he could calculate how far he was east or west of it. He might indeed carry out a clock which should always tell Greenwich time. But how could he tell whether his clock had gone correctly? And how convenient would it be if there were in the heavens a clock, furnished with a dial-plate and hands, which always marked Greenwich time, and by which a mariner could always set his chronometer!

The clocks we are accustomed to have a set of

* That is to say he can determine when his *clock* should point to twelve at noon, according to a rule by which the time can be computed with perfect accuracy. The reader will remember that the sun moves a little quicker at one time than at another, as indicated by the almanack entries, "Clock with Sun," "Clock before Sun," &c.

numbers, from I to XII, arranged round a dial; in the centre of which a pair of hands are fastened, which turn with a regular motion, telling the time by passing over the different figures. As children we find some difficulty in "learning the clock," but once learnt we can easily find out from it the exact time of day.

If the figures were placed very irregularly over the dial, and if the clock's hands moved somewhat more quickly at one time than at another, we should find out what o'clock it was with more trouble. Still we might manage to use such a clock if we had a correct table written out of the time indicated by the different irregularly placed figures, and if we were well acquainted with the mechanism of the clock, and knew when it was to be expected to gain or lose a little.

Now there *is* such a clock to be seen on any clear and moonlight night,—" the visible surface of the starry heavens." The stars are the fixed marks upon it, and the Moon is the moveable hand, as in its monthly circuit round the Earth it passes in front of some stars and hides them, and glides beside and between others, with a movement which is not under all circumstances uniform.

"That the Moon does so move among the stars while the latter hold constantly, with respect to each other, the same relative position, the notice of a few nights, or even hours, will satisfy the commencing student." We may chance to look out some evening in early spring, and see the Moon setting along with "the Pleiades." The next evening, when the Pleiades are setting at nearly the same hour, we shall see that the Moon has moved to stars a great deal higher up; and in a fortnight when the Pleiades are setting, the Moon may be seen in almost the opposite part of the firmament.

Every principal star that it will pass during the month is carefully noted down, with the apparent distance of each from the Moon, are noted down with the utmost care and precision in an almanack prepared at the national expense.*

But we have not explained *all* the inconvenience of this vast clock. 'Suppose the clock with irregular figures, and hands with a motion not quite uniform, had the additional awkwardness of having its hands raised up several inches from the dial-plate, so that we could not read the correct time, unless we happened to stand exactly opposite the clock, this would give us additional trouble; for if we were *obliged* to look at the clock from above or below, or from one side, we should have to note the exact position from which we saw the clock, and from thence calculate what figure the hands point to, if we *could* stand opposite to them.

And just such a calculation must be made when the Moon's movements among the stars are observed. For the Moon is so much nearer to us than the stars are, that two people in very different parts of the Earth will not see the Moon in exactly the same direction, though the difference is not very perceptible. So the observer must always calculate how the Moon would appear if we could view it from the centre of the Earth.

* 'The Nautical Almanack.'

"Such a clock," says Sir John Herschel, "might no doubt be considered a very bad one." But he adds, that if it were our *only* one, and that it were important we should know the time, no pains would be spared to make it easy to *read* it correctly. Accordingly, tables have been made by which true time can be calculated from observations of the Moon's place.

And whether the voyager is in the midst of the wide Pacific, in the frozen North, or steering for the Antipodes, he has only to observe carefully the Moon's distance from some neighbouring star, making the proper allowance for his viewing it from the surface of the earth, not from the centre, and then consult his almanack to see at *what o'clock in Greenwich time* the Moon is at the given distance from that star. By comparing this hour of the day with the actual time in his then present position, he sees how much one time is faster than the other, and thus ascertains exactly how far east or west he may have proceeded.

The Moon, we have seen, is very much nearer than the stars, and can be seen in slightly different directions, from different parts of the Earth. Its distance can therefore be ascertained. Two astronomers, one in England, one at the Cape of Good Hope, observe it. They know the distance from England to the Cape, and having found how much the lines drawn from each station to the centre of the Moon slope towards each other, they know at what distance from the Earth such lines must meet at a point. The result gives two hundred and thirty-seven thousand miles as the Moon's distance.

The Moon.

It is a long way. The passage to the farthest of our colonies, sixteen thousand miles, generally takes, with average winds, four months. But if there could be an ocean highway to the Moon, such a ship must sail steadily for *five years* before reaching its destination. It is a wide space; but how amazing is the thought, that there *would not be room in such a space* for the body of the Sun! Not only so; if we were to imagine the globe of the Sun entirely hollowed out, and the Earth placed in its centre, there would still be room for the Moon's entire path, and an unoccupied space of 204,000 miles in diameter all round.*

Diameter of the Sun, 882,000 miles.

Diameter of the Moon's orbit, 474,000 miles.

THE EARTH AND MOON.

Scale, one twelfth of an inch to eight thousand miles. To represent the sun correctly on this scale, it should be nine inches and one sixth in diameter, and placed at a distance of eighty-two feet five inches and seven twelfths of an inch.

---

* Herschel's 'Treatise,' p. 214.

CHAPTER V.

ECLIPSES OF THE SUN AND MOON.

THESE striking phenomena are always viewed with interest, at the somewhat unfrequent periods of their occurrence. Even the field labourer pauses awhile, spade in hand, to gaze upward at the Sun, so strangely transformed for the time into a sharp crescent; or, if the eclipse be of the Moon, he watches its progress in the quiet and repose of evening, not without an expressed misgiving that the Moon may *suffer* by what befalls it!

We will suppose our readers to be acquainted in a general way with the theory of eclipses. If so, they do not need to be told that the Moon occasionally travels between the Earth and the Sun, thus causing a solar eclipse, or that it is also liable to plunge into the shadow of the Earth, when it, the Sun, and Earth are in a straight line, or nearly so; and thus become eclipsed itself.

A considerable number of our readers will possess the additional information that eclipses of the Sun can only happen at the time of new Moon, while lunar eclipses are possible only when our satellite is full. And a few, on little consideration, especially if they have read some remarks near the commencement of

Chapter III, will rightly explain the non-occurrence of eclipses at *every* new and full Moon, by the fact that the paths of the Earth and Moon not being in the same plane, the Sun, Moon, and Earth are seldom placed in a perfectly straight line on those occasions; or even in a line sufficiently near to being straight, to produce at least a partial eclipse.

But we imagine that the question, " How are eclipses *predicted ?*" would seldom meet a satisfactory answer. Only that custom has made us familiar with the fact, how strange it seems that the almanacks should foretell the eclipses for the coming year, as confidently as they give us the dates of the forthcoming country fairs, or mark December 25th as Christmas Day! Another remarkable fact is, that even the ancients had a method of calculating eclipses. We shall state in as few words as possible their method, and that pursued in the present day.

The ancients, who had nearly everything to learn with respect to the movements of the Sun and planets, followed the excellent plan of narrowly observing the heavens during a long course of years. By doing this they discovered that at certain regular intervals, a set of eclipses observed at one date would occur again. The most useful "cycle" of this sort which they established, was called the Saros, and consisted of eighteen years and eleven days.* It was very nearly accurate, and lunar eclipses could be foretold by it with a considerable degree of certainty.

A lunar eclipse is a real phenomenon, a real darken-

* Nichol's 'Cyclopædia,' p. 214.

ing of the Moon's face for the time being, and therefore visible from an entire hemisphere of the Earth. A solar eclipse, on the other hand, is an event seen only from a comparatively small part of the Earth, and its appearance at a given time entirely depends on the geographical position of the spectator.* For instance, on September 7th, 1858, there was a total eclipse of the Sun to the inhabitants of part of South America. The Sun was completely obscured shortly before three o'clock in the afternoon, Greenwich time, but no eclipse whatever was to be seen that day from the British Isles, or any part of Europe. The Sun's disc was clear as usual. The comparative nearness and small size of the Moon cause this difference. The subject has been illustrated in the following way:—A screen held before a candle may be an eclipse of the candle for one person in the room, but not for another, on account of their difference of place; this illustrates the solar eclipse. But a ball rolled up into a dark corner of the room may be invisible to all the persons in the room at the same time; this represents an eclipse of the Moon.†

It is not believed that the ancients succeeded well in predicting solar eclipses, owing to the limited nature of this phenomenon. They could only foretell that such an occurrence would be visible from *some* part of the Earth.‡

In modern times the cycle is dispensed with, and astronomers calculate from accurately-prepared tables

* Nichol's 'Cyclopædia,' p. 221.
† 'Penny Cyclopædia,' article "Sun" (Eclipse of the).
‡ Nichol's 'Cyclopædia,' p. 221.

of the places of the heavenly bodies, formed by repeated observations through a long course of years, in which allowance is carefully made for all known causes of delay or acceleration.*

The appearance of a total lunar eclipse, as *viewed in the Moon*, would be that of a *great eclipse of the Sun*. In this case our Earth would be the eclipsing body, and would appear so large that the eclipse would be universal over that hemisphere of the Moon. Its duration, too, would be very great, but might be somewhat relieved in its intense darkness by the illuminating power of the Earth's atmosphere.†

A partial eclipse of the Moon would appear as a total eclipse of the Sun to those regions which we observe under shadow (Plate I, fig. 1), and partial to the remainder of the disc. A fainter shade, called the penumbra, always surrounds the darker central shadow, and is caused by the Sun's disc being only partially concealed from the regions thus obscured.‡

We now proceed to consider some of the phenomena of solar eclipses. The Earth and Moon move in orbits, not circular, but slightly elliptical. Consequently, the Earth is at some times of the year a little farther from the Sun than at others; and accordingly the Sun appears somewhat smaller than at the periods when the Earth is nearest to it. The Moon from a similar cause measures more on some days than on others. Should the Moon be at its nearest and the Sun at its farthest

* Nichol's 'Cyclopædia,' p. 214.
† Breen's 'Planetary Worlds,' p. 122.
‡ Herschel's 'Treatise,' p. 225.

at the time of a solar eclipse, the Sun will be completely covered, and the darkness will last more than six minutes.* But should the Moon not happen to be at its nearest, the eclipse will either be momentary, what is called "total without continuance,"† or it will be "annular," a part of the Sun's disc projecting as a brilliant ring of light around the dark body of the Moon.

If we imagine an observer from a distant planet, or from the dark side of the Moon, gazing at our globe during a total eclipse of the Sun, the appearance seen would be that of the greater part of the Earth's disc in bright illumination, but marked with a small black spot, (the Moon's shadow), travelling rapidly over its surface, and causing total eclipse in succession to the inhabitants of each country over which it glided.‡

The width of this round shadow in the longest total eclipse is about one hundred and eighty miles. Its rate of travelling over the Earth (owing to the Moon's real motion, and the Earth's two movements of rotation and revolution,) was calculated by the celebrated Dr. Halley, as having been fifty-nine geographical miles per minute, in the case of the total solar eclipse of 1715; yet an observer of that very eclipse declares that from the top of a belfrey in Lincolnshire, he saw the two sides of the "shadow coming from afar."§

* That is provided the three bodies are in a perfectly straight line, and that the eclipse consequently is "central." Grant's 'History of Physical Astronomy,' p. 362.
† Letter to the 'Times,' by Mr. Hind, March, 1858.
‡ Nichol's 'Cyclopædia,' p. 219.
§ Arago's 'Lectures on Astronomy,' p. 48.

CHAPTER VI.

MERCURY AND VENUS.

OF the five visible planets, these two are naturally classed together, (as observed from the Earth,) from the circumstance of their moving around the Sun in orbits, altogether included in that of our planet. The consequence of their doing so, is that they are never seen in any part of the heavens which is very different from that occupied by the Sun. Moreover they exhibit phases like the Moon, and on rare occasions, when in a straight line between the Earth and the Sun, they cross the Sun's disc, or as astronomers express it, a "transit" takes place, the planet appearing as a round black spot.*

It has always been a matter of difficulty to make out much of their structure. They shine with a dazzling lustre, which has the effect of exaggerating every imperfection of the telescope employed; and it would seem from the recorded observations of those astronomers who have examined them, that they have been, on the whole, seen about as well as the Moon is with the naked eye.

When in crescent-shape, or semicircular, their inner edges are evidently ragged like that of the Moon, owing most probably to the presence of mountains and

* Airy's 'Lectures,' p. 149.

valleys. There are also faintly shaded spots on the illuminated part, but so faint are they, and so liable to change, that the natural conclusion is, "that we do not see, as in the Moon, the real surface of these planets, but only their atmospheres, much loaded with clouds, and which may serve to mitigate the otherwise intense glare of their sunshine."*

But even this slight variation of their brightness is sufficient, when viewed from day to day, to acquaint us with the fact of their rotation on their axes. By taking an average from a great number of rotations, the day of Mercury has been estimated at twenty-four hours five minutes, and that of Venus at twenty-three hours, twenty-one minutes, and twenty-two seconds, of our time.†

Having spoken of the general points of resemblance in these "inferior planets," so called in contradistinction to the "superior" planets, which are situated outside the orbit of the Earth, we will now treat of them separately.

MERCURY has been viewed with interest from the earliest times, and under various names has been worshipped by the heathen nations of antiquity. Yet it is related that Copernicus, who lived to attain his seventieth year, never once succeeded in seeing Mercury, and on his death-bed much regretted the fact.‡ His horizon was generally rendered obscure by mists rising from the Vistula.§

* Herschel's 'Treatise,' p. 279.
† Nichol's 'Cyclopædia,' pp. 494, 767.
‡ 'Cosmos,' vol. iii, p. 347.
§ Breen's 'Planetary Worlds,' p. 129.

The planet is detected more easily in tropical latitudes than elsewhere,* owing to the short duration of twilight, a result of the comparatively vertical position of the Sun.

"The sun's rim dips—the stars rush out,
At one stride comes the dark."†

With a tolerably clear horizon, however, Mercury may be observed even in our latitudes for a few days every year. We scan the almanack, till we find a morning in which Mercury rises nearly two hours before the Sun, or an evening in which its setting follows that of the Sun by a similar interval. The morning twilight is perhaps preferable, as the observer can watch for the rising of the planet, and note its expected place with regard to two or three bright stars. When this is carefully done, the sudden emerging of the glittering planet above the horizon is a striking sight, and it can then be watched into broad daylight, when it will appear like a very small miniature of the Moon. (Plate VI, fig. 1.) If sought for in the evening, the most likely time to find it is when some conspicuous planets, such as Venus or Jupiter, happen to be in the western portion of the sky, as they will come in sight in the twilight sooner than any of the fixed stars, and with the help of a sketch made beforehand by means of the almanack, will serve as a guide to the position of Mercury.

Mercury's diameter, as stated by Herschel,‡ is about

* Nichol's 'Cyclopædia,' p. 494.
† Coleridge's 'Ancient Mariner.'
‡ Herschel's 'Treatise,' p. 278.

three thousand two hundred miles; its average distance from the Sun upwards of thirty-six millions of miles; and its year is about the length of three of our months.

The apparent size of Mercury, dependent on its distance from the Earth, varies from five to twelve seconds. That is to say, if we call the two opposite points of our horizon one hundred and eighty degrees, Mercury at its largest would appear only one-fifth of a minute in diameter; a minute being the sixtieth part of a degree.

The apparent average diameter of the Moon is thirty minutes. A telescope therefore which showed the Moon of the size represented in Plate III, would exhibit Mercury no larger than the mountain marked as "Pico," near the upper edge of the Moon.

The nearest approach which Mercury makes to the Earth, is about fifty millions of miles; that being of course at the period when it is nearly between us and the Sun.

VENUS, on the other hand, sometimes comes within twenty-eight millions of miles of the Earth. No other planet comes so near, and as it goes farther away than Mercury, when situated at the far side of the Sun, the variations in its apparent size are very striking.

Like Mercury, when viewed through the telescope, it shows all the successive changes of form, which "to the naked eye are characteristic of nothing but the Moon."* (Plate VI, figs. 2, 3, 4.)

Its time of greatest brightness is far from being that of its appearing "full." It will be seen from the figure

* 'Penny Cyclopædia,' p. 248.

that its whole diameter, as observed from the Earth, is smallest at that time. As it travels in its orbit to the position corresponding to "half moon," its apparent brightness increases, and the planet attains its greatest brilliancy when at a distance of forty degrees from the Sun.* After this point, though the planet's apparent diameter increases, it becomes less and less conspicuous to the naked eye, owing to the illuminated crescent becoming extremely narrow. The narrow crescent, as seen on February 22nd, is a singular object in a telescope, and rendered still more so by the tremulous motion of the atmosphere, which usually causes an object to "boil," as astronomers express it, when viewed near the horizon.

There is a beautiful tradition respecting the phases of Venus, which appears, however, to partake rather of the nature of an allegory or illustration, than of a historical anecdote. It is said that when Copernicus announced his theory of the solar system, it was objected that were his theory true, Venus ought at certain positions of its orbit, to exhibit the various forms of the Moon. The invention of the telescope had not then been dreamt of; but it is said that Copernicus, in a fine spirit of prophecy answered, that should men ever see Venus better, they would discern these phases. No mention is made of this story by Galileo, who discovered the varying forms of Venus in the year 1611, with the aid of the telescope; or by Gassendi, the biographer of Copernicus. Copernicus, indeed, was not spared to answer any objections to his

* Nichol's 'Cyclopædia,' p. 767.

system, as he barely lived to lay his hand upon a copy of his own work, and never opened it.*

In that work he is not altogether silent on the subject, and in fact, proposes a different theory to account for the circumstance of Mercury and Venus always appearing circular; namely, that these near neighbours of the Sun are possibly self-luminous, or completely saturated with the solar rays.*

The transits of the planet Mercury occur about fourteen times in a century, those of Venus far more rarely, owing to the greater length of its year, and its consequently coming less frequently into that part of its orbit situated between the Earth and the Sun. Were its orbit and that of the Earth in precisely the same plane, the transit would occur at every return of Venus to that position. The orbits are, however, very much inclined to each other, and it very seldom happens that Venus is sufficiently near to the point "where their planes intersect," at the time of its coming to the position corresponding to the new Moon. The first transit recorded as having been observed was in 1639. Only two have occurred since then, namely, in 1761 and 1769; and there will not be another till the year 1874.†

These transits of Venus are especially remarkable for the use which has been made of them in ascertaining the distance of the Sun from the Earth; and thereby, deducing the real dimensions of the whole Solar System.

* 'Penny Cyclopædia,' article "Venus."
† Ibid., article "Transit."

The working out of this problem in all its bearings must be classed among the complicated subjects of Astronomy; but the *principle* of it is pronounced by Sir John Herschel to be " very simple and obvious."*

In Professor Airy's " Six Lectures on Astronomy," this interesting problem is unfolded in a manner sufficiently clear for the understanding of *any* reader who will bring a little careful attention to the subject. As we could not give a complete explanation of the matter without copying *verbatim* from Airy's work, we shall merely state some of the leading facts of the case, referring our readers to the " Six Lectures " to ascertain the use which has been made of them.†

1st.—The dimensions of the Earth, and the distance in miles between any two points on its surface, are accurately known.

2nd.—The *proportion* which the distance of Venus from the Sun bears to its distance from the Earth, may be accurately ascertained by observing how much Venus can go to the right or left of the Sun. By making a diagram of the two orbits, that is, of the Earth and of Venus, it will be found that to represent the state of things in which Venus moves away to the distance of forty-seven degrees and no more, of the celestial vault on either side of the Sun, the distances must be laid down in the *proportion* of about two and a half to one.

The reader who does not easily understand this statement, may perhaps make it clearer to himself by

* Herschel's 'Treatise,' p. 256.
† Airy's ' Six Lectures,' pp. 132, 140.

drawing two lines at an angle of ninety-four degrees, that is, twice forty-seven, E being the place of the Earth, and V, V, (equi-distant from E,) the places of Venus. Let him erect perpendiculars at V, V, and at their intersection mark S for the place of the Sun. Then, with S as centre and the distance S V as radius, let him describe a circle; that will be the orbit of Venus; and, with the same centre, and the distance

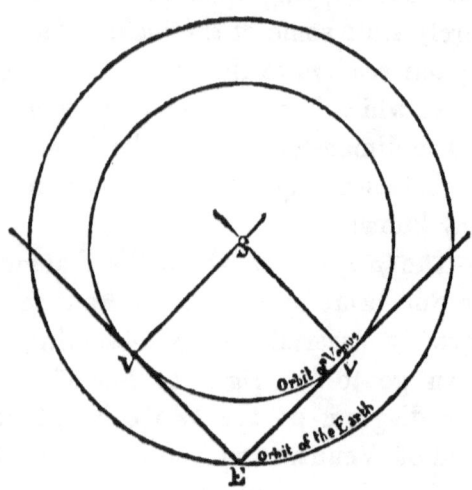

S E for radius, let him describe another circle; that will be the orbit of the Earth. He will then find by measurement that the distance of the Sun from the orbit of Venus, will be to the distance of the orbit of Venus from the orbit of the Earth, in the proportion two and a half to one, nearly, on whatever scale the drawing may be made. This plan of ascertaining the

Mercury and Venus.

proportions of the planets' distances was known to the ancient astronomers.

An acquaintance with this *proportion* is quite another affair from a knowledge of the absolute *distances* of Venus or the Sun. That was the point which remained to be solved.

3rd.—Venus being much nearer to us than to the Sun, the distances as we have said being in the proportion of one to two and a half, it follows that two observers on two widely distant parts of the Earth, would, at the time of transit, see the planet on slightly different parts of the Sun's disc. The planet in each case would traverse in a straight line, and the *distance* between the two straight lines thus observed (being, as we may remark without going deeper into the subject, a known *distance*, that is, of two places on the Earth, multiplied by a known *proportion*, that is, of the distance between Venus and the Earth, and Venus and the Sun, thereby showing an *actually measured space on the Sun's disc*) is the really important thing in the whole observation.*

This distance was ascertained with beautiful accuracy, by noting the *time* occupied in the transit of Venus, as observed at each place.

The method of ascertaining the Sun's distance by a simultaneous observation from various parts of the Earth, of the transit of Venus, was recommended by Halley, when upwards of eighty years of age, and nearly twenty years before the transit of 1761. He be-

---

* Herschel's 'Treatise,' p. 257.

queathed the observation of this transit, and that of 1769, as a task to posterity.

Accordingly, as 1761 approached, various astronomers were sent to distant parts of the Earth to view the transit, but cloudy weather hindered or injured the greater part of the observations.* There remained, however, the chance of 1769, according to the curious cycle of these phenomena which run in *pairs*, separated by only eight years, and then divided by intervals of one hundred and twenty-two and one hundred and five years alternately.†

The hopes of astronomers fondly turned to 1769, and "expeditions were fitted out on the most efficient scale, by the British, French, Russian, and other governments, for the express purpose of performing the observation."‡ The celebrated expedition of Captain Cook, to Otaheite, was one of them.

We can imagine the interest, the intelligent excitement, with which each group of observers in their isolated nooks of the Earth, must have awaited the approach of June 3rd, 1769; the solemn feeling with which on that clouldless day, for so it happily proved in most places, they saw the first "notch" on the eastern border of the Sun, made by the advancing planet; the calm sensation as of victory, when after upwards of five hours the moment of its departure was correctly noted; and then the months of expectation (before steam packets, railroads, and electric telegraphs

---

* 'Penny Cyclopædia,' p. 135.
† Nichol's 'Cyclopædia,' p. 768.
‡ Herschel's 'Treatise,' p. 259.

were!) to find how their labours were appreciated at home, how other observers had fared, and what result would be obtained from a comparison of the whole series.

The most useful of all the observations were those made by Captain Cook, at Otaheite, and by the Danish observers at Wardhoe, in Lapland, near the North Cape.*

Venus varies in apparent diameter from about one minute (one sixtieth of a degree) to only ten seconds. Its real diameter is stated by Herschel as seven thousand eight hundred miles; its year is upwards of seven of our months, and its average distance from the Sun, as ascertained at the transit of 1769, more than sixty-eight millions of miles.

This beautiful planet has often been clearly visible in daylight. The author has watched for it during sunshine, and easily found it for several successive evenings; and has also traced it till twelve o'clock at noon, at a time when its rising preceded that of the Sun.†

Venus has also been occasionally observed, both as a morning and evening star, to cast a pretty strong shadow. Late in the evening of January 24th, 1854, when both Sun and Moon were sufficiently out of the way, the planet Venus being in its position of greatest brilliancy, shone with a remarkable lustre. We ob-

* Airy's 'Lectures,' p. 139.
† In January, 1851. On this occasion the author showed Venus, through the telescope, to several passers-by, who invariably thought the glasses of the instrument were removed or useless, and that they saw the Moon.

served it in a room with a single window, every sash of which was imaged on the ground, as it would have been in moonlight, and even the slight waves and concentric lines on the panes could be clearly traced. Our Plate VI, fig. 2, shows the form of Venus on this evening.

CHAPTER VII.

MARS.

HAVING already treated of our own planet, the Earth, and its satellite, the Moon, we now proceed to describe the three visible planets, the orbits of which are outside that of the Earth. Of these, our nearest neighbour is Mars. Though it does not approach quite so near to the Earth as Venus does, yet the changes in its apparent diameter are considerable. It always appears red to the naked eye, or rather of a deep orange yellow, but in the distant parts of its orbit it only seems like a tolerably conspicuous star, rather to be discovered from its position than from its brightness. When at its nearest point, on the contrary, it shines with a full steady light, and cannot fail to attract attention.

At such times it can be very successfully observed with powerful telescopes; and as it appears (contrary to a belief held at one time by astronomers) to have but a small atmosphere, it is probable that much of its real surface can on these occasions be seen. Its physical features are therefore better known than those of any of our companion orbs, excepting the Moon.* Several

* Nichol's 'Cyclopædia,' p. 488.

maps of its surface have been drawn, and all concur in showing the clear outlines of what may be continents and oceans, as well as bright spots around the poles, corresponding in all respects to our arctic and antarctic fields of ice.

Those parts of Mars which are conjectured to be land, are of "an ochrey tinge," and the portions believed to be water are greenish.* The axis of Mars inclines to the plane of its orbit to very nearly the same extent as that of the Earth; it is therefore probable that Mars has seasons quite analogous to ours, but of greater length, because the year of Mars is equal to nearly a year and eleven months of our time. The effects of the seasons appear to be very clearly displayed in the white spots of each pole. Each of these "disappear when they have been long exposed to the Sun, and are greatest when just emerging from the long night of their polar winter."† The elder Herschel was the first to point out this agreement between the seasons of Mars and the appearance of its polar regions;‡ and later observers have confirmed the probability of the idea thus expressed by him, that "in these white spots we behold a wintry effect, similar in every respect to the fall of snow upon the Earth at that season."§ Herschel considered also that the Earth would show similar changes if viewed from a distance, only that the variations in the spots would not be so great.‖

* Herschel's 'Treatise,' p. 279.
† Ibid., p. 279.
‡ 'Cosmos,' vol. iii, p. 370.
§ Breen's 'Planetary Worlds,' p. 179.
‖ Ibid., p. 179.

Mars.

It is calculated that Mars turns on its axis in twenty-four hours, thirty-nine minutes, and twenty-one seconds.* Its diameter is about four thousand one hundred miles; it is therefore much smaller than either the Earth or Venus, but larger than Mercury.

The planet Mars will always be viewed by the Astronomer with especial interest, as having led the illustrious Kepler to his grand discovery of the real forms of the planetary orbits. From the times of antiquity it was held that their orbits were of the circular form, and their movements uniform; that is to say, that they always travel at the same pace. But the restless busy mind of man had also from ancient times endeavoured to test this theory by observation. The more accurately observations were made, the more apparent became the fact that the planets *cannot* move in simple circles. Then they invented small circles called "epicycles" travelling on the circumference of large ones called "deferents;" and, fettered by the idea that the Earth, not the Sun, was the centre of the system, endeavoured to reconcile theory with observation by a complication of movement, truly ingenious in the invention of it, but which few would care to follow who are familiar with the truth, in its beauty and simplicity.

The system of Copernicus removed much of this complication. The Sun was now made the centre of the system, and the planets were represented as moving round him in circles. The theory of Copernicus had the peculiar charm belonging to a near approach to

* Herschel's 'Treatise,' p. 280.

truth; it explained the seasons of the Earth, and the occasional retrograde movements of the planets, as well as their movements taken in the average. But, as before, it was soon found that when the positions of the planets were accurately observed at various parts of their orbits, something was wrong in the theory; and Copernicus, hampered with the idea that all planetary motions must be of a circular nature, was obliged to introduce the old complicated epicycles to account for all irregularities.*

About twenty years after the death of Copernicus, the illustrious Tycho Brahe commenced his observations of the heavenly bodies. He carried them on for nearly forty years, having made several improvements in astronomical instruments, and thereby having constructed a series of recorded observations of the places of heavenly bodies, which in his day were of unrivalled accuracy and importance. He had no telescope, that instrument having been invented after his death.

Near the end of Tycho's life he became acquainted with Kepler, then known as the author of a wildly speculative work on the mysteries of creation. Tycho, seeing the ardent thirst after truth implanted in Kepler's nature, as well as the original genius of his mind, strongly advised him in future to build his theories on recorded facts, and he furnished Kepler with his own observations. It is to following this advice that Kepler owes all his fame; but Tycho Brahe did not live to share his triumph.

Tycho Brahe had given great attention to the planet

* 'Penny Cyclopædia,' article "Copernicus."

MARS; and without delay Kepler devoted all the energies of his mind to account for its movements.

The orbit of the planet Mars departs more widely from the circular form than that of any of the visible planets excepting Mercury, and as Mars is much more easily watched than Mercury, its movements are particularly well adapted for investigation.

Eight years after the death of Tycho appeared Kepler's "great and extraordinary book on the 'Motion of Mars,' a work which holds the intermediate place between the works of Copernicus and those of Newton," and contains two of the three famous laws of nature, which will for ever make Kepler's name illustrious.

We shall refer only to the *first* of these laws, although the second, relating to the velocities of the planets, and the third, relating to their distances, and not discovered by Kepler till twelve years afterwards, were both deduced from the movements of the planet Mars.

Kepler's first law was as follows:—Planets move in ellipses, having the Sun in one of their foci. Kind reader, have you any practical acquaintance with the foci of an ellipse? If not, you are ignorant of the scientific manner of laying out an oval flower-bed, and we shall deserve your thanks for expounding it to you. Plant two short upright stakes at equal distances from the centre of the plot of ground which your good taste has decided will be more appropriately occupied by an oval, or rather, an ellipse, than by any other figure. Join together the ends of a piece of cord into a loop, long enough to throw quite loosely around both of the stakes. Then with some pointed tool, say the ferule of a walking-stick, pull the string tight; and then still keeping it stretched, carry the stick round the stakes, tracing its path on the smooth turf as you go along; and when you regain your starting-point you will find that you have described on the ground a beautiful and perfect ellipse. You will have done more: you will have executed a model of a planetary orbit! Take away one of the stakes; the remaining stake now represents the Sun, the common focus of how many planets, with their various ellipses, some, as those of Mars and Mercury, quite sensibly removed from the circular form, and to be traced by planting the "foci" at considerable distances; others, as that of Venus, little different from a circle, and requiring the foci to be in close proximity.

We can study the tables of the planets, and at a glance obtain an idea of their orbits; but to Kepler it was the up-hill work of discovery, with the imperfect methods of his time; like Columbus winning a new world with three fragile barks.

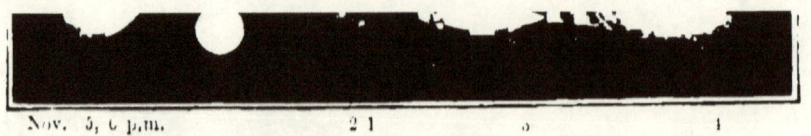

JUPITER AND ITS SATELLITES,
as seen on four successive evenings, in November, 1857.

CHAPTER VIII.

JUPITER.

THE splendid planet Jupiter had been admired and carefully observed for many centuries before any one imagined that it possessed four moons or satellites. This discovery was made by the illustrious Galileo in the year 1610.* The telescope had been only two years invented at that time; and Galileo relates that he frequently directed it to the planets and fixed stars, and observed them "with incredible delight,"—*incredibili animi jucunditate.*†

He was looking through his telescope at Jupiter at one o'clock in the morning of January 7th, 1610, when he observed three small stars near the body of the planet, two to the east and one to the west of it. They were all in a straight line, and he thought that they appeared very bright. But he concluded that they were fixed stars which happened to be in the same direction as the planet.

He looked again at the planet on the 8th, without having any particular motive for doing so, that he could afterwards recollect. The little stars were quite dif-

* 'Martyrs of Science,' p. 25.
† Ibid., p. 23.

ferently arranged; all appeared to the west of Jupiter, and nearer to each other than on the preceding night.

Now the philosopher knew that Jupiter being a planet, was naturally to be expected to change its place among the fixed stars. But Jupiter was according to all calculations *moving to the west* at that time, and how could it then be found to the *east* of the three stars? Yet such was the fact.

Galileo waited for the following night with the utmost anxiety, but was disappointed, for the heavens were wholly veiled in clouds! But on the night of the 10th, he saw the planet again; two only of the stars appeared, both on the east of Jupiter. He now concluded that these stars really moved. On the 11th he still saw two stars, both to the east of Jupiter; but one of them was twice as large as the other (being, no doubt, quite close to a third satellite).. On this night Galileo drew the conclusion from all he had observed, "that there were in the heavens three stars which revolved round Jupiter in the same manner that Venus and Mercury revolve round the Sun." He observed them again on January 12th, and on the 13th he perceived that their number was four.*

Such observations as these are exactly what we could make on several successive nights with our telescope; and very interesting it is to watch the rapid changes of place among these *moons* (Plate VII).

But how deeply impressive must such a discovery have appeared to Galileo! showing that Jupiter resembled our Earth in having "lesser lights to rule the

* 'Martyrs of Science,' p. 27.

Jupiter.

night," and probably to give light to its inhabitants. Besides in the system of Jupiter and its satellites, philosophers saw, as it were, a beautiful *model of the entire solar system;* and could point it out to the many who disbelieved Copernicus's views, as a little world, in which the laws attributed to the solar system were regularly followed.*

Galileo named these satellites after his patrons at Florence, "The Medicean Stars." They have also been called by mythological names, Io, Europa, Ganymede, and Calisto.† But modern astronomers merely speak of them as the first satellite, the second, and so on. Since Galileo's time many curious facts have been made out about these satellites, of which we must presently give an account.

Jupiter is the largest of the planets, its diameter (eighty-seven thousand miles) being eleven times that of the Earth.‡ When viewed through a telescope its disc may be seen crossed in one direction by dark bands or belts. They are by no means alike at all times, varying in their breadth and situation on the disc, but never in their general direction, parallel to Jupiter's equator. They are supposed to be the effect of currents in Jupiter's atmosphere, similar to our trade-winds.§

Jupiter revolves on its axis with surprising quickness, its day and night put together being less than ten hours.‖

* Herschel's 'Treatise,' p. 296.
† 'Cosmos,' vol. ii, p. 316.
‡ Ibid., vol. iii, p. 375.
§ Herschel's 'Treatise,' p. 280.
‖ 'Cosmos,' vol. iii, p. 377.

The Sun appears to Jupiter five times smaller than to us.*

The satellites of Jupiter are very small, compared with the size of the planet round which they revolve. The diameter of our Moon is more than equal to one fourth of the Earth's diameter; whereas Jupiter's diameter is nearly twenty-five times that of its largest satellite, the "third."† The diameter of this satellite is calculated at three thousand three hundred and seventy-seven miles; that of the smallest, the "second," is believed to be two thousand and sixty-eight miles.‡

They revolve round Jupiter with amazing swiftness, the most distant taking but sixteen days, sixteen hours, and thirty-two minutes to complete its revolution, and the nearest but one day, eighteen hours, and twenty-eight minutes. This nearest satellite is upwards of five hundred thousand miles distant from Jupiter; and the fourth, and farthest off satellite is removed more than two millions of miles.§

A spot has been discovered on the disc of the fourth satellite which disappeared and returned at regular intervals, proving that the satellite turns on its axis.‖ The other satellites also appear to have obscure spots on them, of great extent, sufficient to make their discs much duller at one time than at another; that is,

---

* Arago's 'Lectures,' p. 27.
† 'Cosmos,' vol. iii, p. 340.
‡ Herschel's 'Treatise,' p. 295.
§ Ibid., p. 417.
‖ Arago's 'Lectures,' p. 27.

Jupiter.

when they have revolved on their axes so that these obscure spots are turned towards the Earth.*

It is believed that these satellites always turn the same face towards Jupiter, by revolving round it in exactly the same time that they occupy in turning on their axes.* This is precisely similar to what has been remarked of the Moon's motion.

To the inhabitants of Jupiter these moons must constantly present phases, as our Moon does to us. *We* always see Jupiter's moons *round* because they (as well as Jupiter itself) are always to us in the condition of the Moon when full, since the orbit of the Earth is, comparatively speaking, so small, that we always lie nearly in the same direction from Jupiter as the Sun does.†

Some of the four satellites are frequently hidden from our view, being either behind Jupiter or passing in front of it; or else *eclipsed* by passing through Jupiter's shadow.‡ In fact, three of the four satellites owing to their nearness to Jupiter in proportion to its size, are eclipsed every time they go round.§

These eclipses may happen when the satellites are already hidden from our view by being behind the body of the planet. But when this is not the case they may be observed; the satellite disappears without any apparent reason.§

Not long after the discovery of Jupiter's satellites

---

* Herschel's 'Treatise,' p. 293.
† See figure, p. 84.
‡ Herschel's 'Treatise,' p. 292.
§ Airy's 'Lectures,' p. 182.

astronomers found that these eclipses could be observed with great accuracy, and their periods foretold.* They made tables of them with the utmost care, during a long succession of years.†

The consequence of their doing so was a most curious discovery, affecting the whole subject of astronomy. By observing the eclipses of Jupiter's satellites they ascertained the fact that *light travels at a certain rate*, and also *what that rate is*.‡

No one can have failed to observe that *sound* takes some little time to travel. We may see the flash of a gun in a distant ship, but the *report* of it does not reach our ears for several moments. Light, then, moves more swiftly than sound. But how can we tell whether we saw the light in the moment that it really flashed forth?

Galileo felt curious on this point, and tried the following experiment:—He had two lanterns constructed with moveable shades, which could be dropped instantaneously, so as to conceal the light. With one of these he ascended to the top of a mountain, while an

---

* Airy's 'Lectures,' p. 182.

† These eclipses afforded the first astronomical solution ever suggested of the famous problem of the Longitude. Galileo recommended this method in 1612. An observer comparing the *predicted* time of the eclipse with the local time of its occurrence at his then present position, may determine his longitude. The principle is the same as that of the " Lunar Method," described at p. 44. But these eclipses cannot be observed at sea, on account of the difficulty of steadying a telescope while the ship is in motion. For this and other reasons the Lunar Method is the one always employed on voyages.—*Herschel's Treatise*, p. 143 and 296, and *Cosmos*, vol. ii, p. 318.

‡ Herschel's 'Treatise,' p. 297.

assistant by his directions carried the second to the summit of another mountain. This person was desired to fix his eyes on Galileo's lantern, and when he should observe the light disappear, instantly cover up his own.

Galileo thought it possible that some time would elapse between the instant when he dropped his own screen, and that in which he should observe the light of the other lantern disappear. Such was not the case; the two lights disappeared simultaneously, and the philosopher concluded that the transmission of light *occupied no time whatever.** He was mistaken; his experiments had been tried on too small a scale.

In the year 1675 a Danish astronomer named Roemer observed on comparing together several tables of the eclipses of Jupiter's satellites, that these eclipses sometimes occurred *too soon,* that is, sooner than he could have expected by a calculation from their average time, and sometimes they appeared to come *too late.* Yet there was no doubt that the observations had been correctly noted down. On further examining these tables, Roemer discovered that the eclipses always appeared sixteen minutes and twenty-six seconds later when the Earth was at its greatest distance from Jupiter, at c, than when it was at its nearest point, at o.† He pondered for some time on the possible cause,

---

* Arago's 'Lectures,' p. 23.

† It should be understood that in practice the satellites cannot be observed when the earth is at c, because the sun is then in the same direction, and its light overpowers them. When the earth has moved a little way from c, they can again be seen; and the times of their

and came to the conclusion that light takes sixteen minutes and twenty-six seconds to travel across the whole breadth of the Earth's path round the Sun.

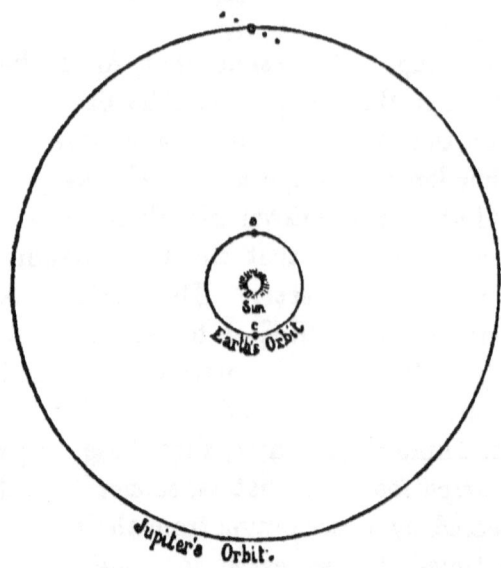

Now the distance of the Sun is known, and the diameter of the Earth's orbit must be twice that amount. It is one hundred and ninety millions of miles; and if light can traverse such a space in sixteen minutes and twenty-six seconds, its rate per second must be one hundred and ninety-two thousand miles.*

This is a startling conclusion; so great a velocity

eclipses are delayed in such a ratio while the earth approaches c, or are hastened as it removes farther from c, as to give the above interval, sixteen minutes and twenty-six seconds, as the delay that would be perceptible were it possible to see the satellites at that time.

* 'Herschel's 'Treatise,' p. 297.

appears almost incredible. But it has received complete confirmation from a remarkable discovery, that of the Aberration of Light, made long after Roemer's time by the astronomer Bradley, who obtained almost exactly the same result by another method, quite unconnected with the satellites of Jupiter.*

* Herschel's 'Treatise,' p. 297.

CHAPTER IX.

SATURN.

THIS planet presents an appearance peculiar to itself, so far as is known. It is surrounded by a broad thin ring, illuminated (as the planets and their satellites also are) by the light of the Sun. The "wooden horizon" of an ordinary artificial globe is not unlike, in its form and relation to the globe, to the ring of Saturn. If, instead of nearly touching the globe, the "horizon" were to be enlarged, so as to be distant one-third of the globe's diameter, if it were itself rather wider than one fourth of the globe's diameter, and if it were made of an exceedingly thin plate of metal, or piece of card, *no thicker than the one hundred and eighty-fifth part of the "horizon's" breadth*, it would make a tolerably correct model of Saturn and its ring.

The resemblance would be increased if a division were made in the "wooden horizon" all the way round, equal to a ninth part of its breadth, thus separating it into two rings, for in fact Saturn has two rings, one within the other, a black line indicating their separation.* The planet turns on its axis in ten hours and a half, as calculated by Sir William Herschel, from observations of certain dusky spots on its surface. He considered

* Herschel's 'Treatise,' p. 282.

SATURN AND ITS SATELLITE "TITAN,"
observed Feb. 15th, 1857.

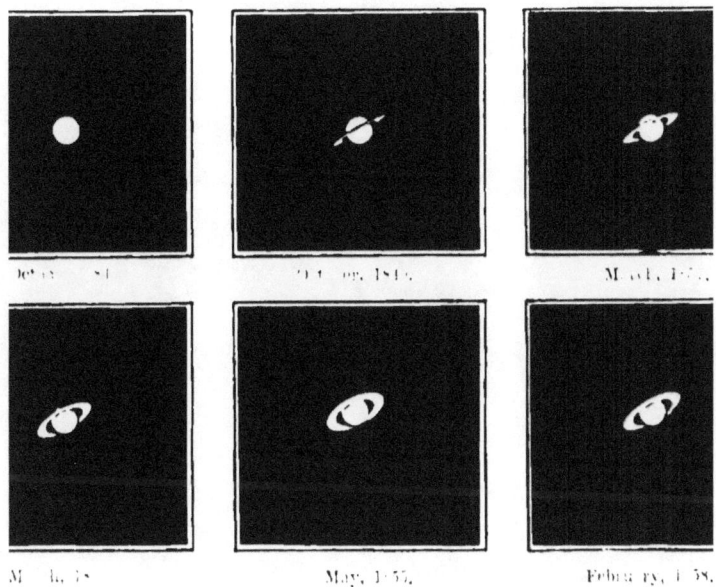

Saturn.

that the rings also revolve in a nearly similar period; such a motion would tend to keep them steadily in their places, nearly in the plane of Saturn's equator.*

In looking through a telescope at this planet astronomers may every fifteen years see a curious spectacle, Saturn without a ring!* (Plate VIII.) Saturn completes its revolution round the Sun in nearly thirty

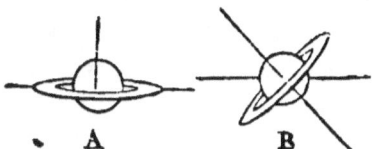

years, turning constantly, as has been said, on its axis, and having its axis always pointing in the same direction, in whatever part of its orbit the planet may be. This direction is not *perpendicular* to the planet's path, as shown at A, but *inclined* to it, B.

The orbit of our Earth is very much smaller than that of Saturn, and is nearly on the same plane.

If we were to stand in the centre of a large room while some person carried a globe in a circle round us, and on a level with our eyes, the globe, if held obliquely, and with its axis steadily pointing in one direction, would in one part of its circuit exhibit a considerable portion of the upper surface of its wooden horizon, in another part an equal portion of the under, and in two points of the circuit, those opposite to each other, both upper and under surfaces of the "horizon" would be invisible, and only its edge would appear.

* Herschel's 'Treatise,' pp. 282—284.

Such an experiment would represent the successive appearances of Saturn as seen from the Earth. But its ring is so extremely thin, thin in proportion to its breadth, and in absolute thickness less than one hundred miles, that it is, when placed exactly edgewise to the Earth, invisible, except perhaps, with telescopes of extraordinary power.*

At such times the *satellites of Saturn* may be most easily observed. Eight of these satellites have been discovered, at very different times, since Saturn was first examined with the telescope.† Like those of Jupiter they are small in comparison to the planet round which they revolve, the diameter of the largest satellite being only one-fifteenth part of the diameter of Saturn. This satellite is the sixth in distance from Saturn. It performs its revolutions in nearly sixteen days. The eighth, or most distant, takes more than seventy-nine days for its monthly circuit, and the first, or nearest, only twenty-two hours and thirty-seven minutes. These eight moons have received the names of Mimas, Enceladus, Tethys, Dione, Rhea, Titan (this is the large one), Hyperion, and Japetus.†

Saturn has bands or belts like those of Jupiter, but less strongly marked and somewhat broader.

There is a remarkable variation in the appearance of Saturn's *polar regions*, dependent on the *seasons of its year*. These regions shine more brightly in their respective winters. It is impossible to say whether

---

* Herschel's 'Treatise,' p. 283.
† 'Cosmos,' vol. iii, p. 386.

this increased brilliancy is owing to the formation of snow and ice, or to an extraordinary accumulation of clouds; but it certainly appears like the effect of a change of weather.*

Saturn's sky must be splendid with eight moons continually changing their places, and with the magnificent rings, which must appear to the inhabitants of "those regions which lie above the enlightened sides, as vast arches spanning the sky from horizon to horizon."† "On the other hand," as Sir John Herschel continues, "in the regions beneath the dark side (of the rings) a solar eclipse of fifteen years in duration under their shadow, must afford (to our ideas) an inhospitable asylum to animated beings, ill compensated by the faint light of the satellites. But we shall do wrong to judge of the fitness or unfitness of their condition from what we see around us, when, perhaps, the very combinations which convey to our minds only images of horror, may be in reality theatres of the most striking and glorious displays of beneficent contrivance."

The story of the discovery of Saturn's rings is scarcely less interesting than that of Galileo's first observations of the satellites of Jupiter.

Before the close of the year 1610 Galileo observed Saturn through a telescope, of the very small size of which such instruments were then constructed. He observed that its form was not round, but rather, as he explained, "like three o's, namely, o O o, the

---

* 'Cosmos,' vol. iii, p. 382.
† Herschel's 'Treatise,' p. 286.

central one being larger than those on each side of it."*

He chose to publish his discovery in *an enigma*, that he might be known as the first discoverer. The enigma appeared a mere confused heap of letters. It was known to be a description of some new fact in astronomy, and contemporary astronomers were thus invited to declare whether they had observed any new phenomena in the heavens. The solution of this enigma was,—"I have discovered that the most distant planet is triple."*

The structure of Saturn's rings was not further explained for more than forty years after. Hevelius described, in 1656, the variations in the form of Saturn, the unequal opening of the "handles," as he called them, and their occasional entire disappearance.†

But the merit of having explained scientifically all the phenomena of Saturn's ring belongs to Huygens (1655). He concealed his discoveries in an enigma or anagram, which he published in 1656. The anagram was as follows:—" aaaaaaa ccccc d eeeee g h iiiiiii llll mm nnnnnnnnn oooo pp q rr s ttttt uuuuu."

He did not explain this anagram till 1659. It contains in Latin, a very happy description of Saturn's ring. "Annulo cingitur, tenui, plano, nusquam cohærente, ad eclipticum inclinato."—" He is surrounded with a ring, thin, plane, nowhere adhering, and inclined to the ecliptic."‡

---

* 'Martyrs of Science,' p. 35.
† 'Cosmos,' vol. ii, p. 318.
‡ 'North British Review,' vol. vii, p. 241.

In 1684 Dominic Cassini first recognised its division into two concentric rings, indicated, as before mentioned, by a black line.* Thinner black lines have since been observed, but they do not appear to have been permanent, and astronomers do not speak confidentially of more than *two* rings, that is, *luminous* ones.† So lately as 1850, a faintly-illuminated *third ring* has been discovered in the space between the planet and the inner ring, and lying in the same plane.‡

* 'Cosmos,' vol. ii, p. 319.
† Ibid., vol. iii, p. 382.
‡ Ibid., p. 383.

CHAPTER X.

COMETS.

THESE extraordinary and as yet imperfectly understood objects scarcely lie within the province of our little treatise, which chiefly undertakes to describe such appearances as are ordinarily to be observed in the heavens. Still, as a comet *sometimes* appears visible to the naked eye,—and the grand and unexpected visitor of 1858 will long be remembered,—we shall offer a few general remarks on the subject, and also make allusion to five or six comets, which may have been seen by some of the readers of this book.

The number of comets is believed to be very great.* Their apppearance has been recorded from remote antiquity; several hundreds have been described, and the illustrious Kepler compared the numbers which probably exist to the multitude of "fishes in the sea."†

Of telescopic comets, there are now discovered, on an average, at least two or three every year.† Comets visible to the naked eye are of comparatively rare occurrence. Twelve were seen in the seventeenth

---

* Herschel's 'Treatise,' p. 300.
† 'Cosmos,' vol. iii, p. 398.

THE COMET OF 185-, (DONATI'S,)
and neighbouring stars, October 11th., 18-8, at 7.2 p. m.

century, eight in the eighteenth, and nine in the first half of the present century.*

The usual appearance of a comet consists of a "nucleus" or head, more or less bright, though indistinct in outline, environed by a faint cloudy atmosphere, and attended by a still fainter cloudy appearance, called the "tail," extending linearly, often through an immense space. The comet of April, 1854, and the remarkable comet of 1858, Donati's, Plate IX, exemplify this description. Some few comets have however appeared divested of a tail; and others have been observed with no trace of nucleus.†

Previous to the discovery of the law of universal gravitation, comets were looked upon as a lawless class of bodies " of whose motions it was quite impossible to take account. By some philosophers they were regarded as meteors kindled into a blaze by the earth's atmosphere."‡

The law of gravitation, however, supplied a clue even to the movements of these wanderers. Newton established the following theory concerning them; that their motions are regulated by the same general laws as those of the planets, and that some of them move in curves of the elliptical form, having the Sun "in one of the *foci* of the ellipse."§

The elliptical paths of comets differ, however, from those of planets, in being more elongated, sometimes to

* 'Cosmos,' vol. iii, p. 398.
† Nichol's 'Cyclopædia,' p. 132.
‡ Mitchell's 'Orbs of Heaven,' p. 148.
§ See page 75.

such an extravagant degree as to cause the comet to approach astonishingly near to the Sun, in one part of its course, and to recede to an enormous distance in another. Where the orbit of a comet is not elliptic, it is a hyperbola, a curve which does not, like the ellipse, return into itself, but on the contrary, branches away to infinity, so that comets whose paths are of this form, visit us but once.*

Many more comets, however, have been proved to travel in the ellipse than in the hyperbola.†

Newton's devoted follower, Dr. Halley, after an elaborate calculation of the path of a comet which appeared in 1682, ascertained that this comet was identical with one noticed twice before, namely, in the years 1531 and 1607. He then thoroughly relying on that principle of order which Newton had detected amid the complicated movements of the heavenly bodies, hazarded the prophecy that after a lapse of seventy-five or seventy-six years, this comet would return. Knowing that he himself would die long before the arrival of that period, he expressed a hope that when the comet should appear, posterity would remember that this first prediction had been made by an Englishman.†

The comet accordingly did re-appear in the year 1758, in December, reached its point nearest the Sun in March 1759, and then receded, gradually disappearing in the distance.‡

---

* Herschel's 'Treatise,' p. 307.
† Nichol's 'Cyclopædia,' p. 132.
‡ Ibid., p. 133.

The exact period for its return is rendered a matter of most difficult calculation by the attraction of the large planets, especially Jupiter and Saturn. Two celebrated mathematicians of the eighteenth century, Clairaut and Lalande, with the assistance of Madame Lepaute, undertook the laborious task of this calculation as the comet's expected return approached. During six months they calculated from morning to night, and computed the distance of each of the two planets, Jupiter and Saturn, from the comet separately for every degree, for one hundred and fifty years.*

The period came on rapidly before the calculations were quite finished, and Clairaut, in announcing that the comet would probably reach its nearest point to the Sun on April 13th, 1759, confessed that he might be in error to the amount of a whole month. The comet reached that point on March 12th. The error was certainly small, only one month in an orbit of seventy-six years.

But when another period of seventy years had fulfilled its course, science had to reach still greater triumphs. The comet re-appeared in 1835. The attraction of the planet Uranus could now be taken into account; and the respective weights of Jupiter and Saturn were better known than in the days of Clairaut. Accordingly, after an absence of seventy-five years, this comet re-appeared within *five days* of its predicted time.† Since then, the planet Neptune has been revealed; and when this comet again returns (in 1911),

---

* 'Orbs of Heaven,' p. 151.
† Nichol's 'Cyclopædia,' p. 133.

it is not likely the error of calculation will exceed as many hours.*

This comet, most justly named *Halley's*, was the first proved to belong to the solar system. There are now six others, the periods of which have been ascertained during the present century.*

They are all visible only in the telescope, and are remarkable for the smallness of their orbits, which notwithstanding their elliptical shape, are entirely included within that of Neptune. "Encke's Comet," the first discovered of these small bodies, performs its revolution in the short period of three years and one hundred and nine days. The five others perform their revolution as follows:†—De Vico's in five years and one hundred and seventy-one days; Brorsen's five years and two hundred and fourteen days; D'Arrest's six years and one hundred and sixty-three days; Biela's six years and two hundred and twenty-seven days; Faye's seven years and one hundred and sixty-three days.

Of the above comets, Encke's, Biela's, and Faye's, have been clearly visible at the predicted times of their approach to the Sun.‡ De Vico's was not thoroughly identified at the period of its expected return in 1855; and Brorsen's does not seem to have been observed in 1851, when it was due. It, however, appeared at its next period, on March 18th, 1857;§ and later in the same

* Nichol's 'Cyclopædia,' p. 133.
† 'Cosmos,' vol. iii, p. 410.
‡ Loomis's 'Recent Progress of Astronomy,' p. 138.
§ 'Illustrated London Almanack' for 1858.

year, the keen eye of Mr. Maclear detected D'Arrest's Comet punctually returning after an absence of upwards of six years. He observed it from the Cape of Good Hope, in spite of a confusing mass of "driblets from the Table Cap," which lay nearly in the line of sight.*

Encke's Comet is remarkable for the gradual contracting of its orbit, a fact not yet thoroughly explained;† and Biela's Comet astonished the astronomers in 1846 by separating into two parts, in which double condition it has ever since remained, and been seen as two widely-separated comets.‡

There are four other telescopic comets, the periods of which are supposed to be under six years; two others with probable revolutions of twelve and fifteen years, and four with periods of between seventy and eighty years.§

The beautiful comet of 1811, of which most of us have (like the author) at least a *traditional* knowledge, is

---

* "Letter from Mr. Maclear to the Astronomer Royal," dated Royal Observatory, Cape of Good Hope, Dec. 26th, 1857. From the Royal Astronomical Society's 'Monthly Notice' for April, 1858.

† 'Orbs of Heaven,' p. 156-8. It has been suggested that the shortening of the period of Encke's Comet may be caused by the existence in space of a "resisting medium" (an idea which had often formed the subject of speculation, even before the discovery of this argument in its favour). "More extensive indications of such a medium must," however, "be discovered, before the problem of its existence can be considered as having received a definite solution. It has not affected to a sensible extent any of the other celestial bodies, and until such (effect) is found to take place, the question relative to it must remain in abeyance."—*Grant's Astronomy*, p. 135.

‡ 'Orbs of Heaven,' p. 144-5.
§ Nichol's 'Cyclopædia, p. 133.

supposed to travel to so enormous a distance from the Sun, that it might possibly take three thousand years to complete its revolution.* Nor is this the longest period that has been assigned to a comet. It is not, however, believed that all comets which have been observed, belong to the Sun. Sweeping through space, they have (it is supposed) been influenced by the Sun's attraction, bent round it, and then quitted its viciuity for ever. Even those which belong to our system may, in the first instance, have had their paths converted into ellipses by the joint influence of the Sun and planets.†

Comets move in a great variety of directions, and are accordingly by no means restricted like the planets‡ to the zodiac; in other words, their orbits often lie in planes much inclined to that of the Earth's orbit.

For instance, Halley's Comet was seen in the year 1835, near the northern boundary of the constellation of Ursa Major, where no known *planet* could possibly have appeared. Another peculiarity is, that the motions of comets, unlike those of planets, are as frequently from east to west as in the opposite or "direct" course.

The alterations of climate through which a comet passes are truly marvellous. The comet of 1680 passed so close to the Sun (within one hundred and fifty thousand miles), that the disc of that luminary must

---

* Nichol's 'Cyclopædia,' p. 133.
† Ibid., p. 134.
‡ That is, the larger planets; for many of the Asteroids travel out of the zodiac during a portion of their orbits; and have hence been often styled the "ultra zodiacal" planets.

(had any eye been there to see it) have appeared to extend from the horizon nearly to the zenith, while at the farthest point of its orbit, the Sun's apparent dimensions will dwindle to half the average breadth of Mars, as seen from the Earth.*

The Sun appears to exercise an extraordinary influence over comets during their brief sojourn in the vicinity of his beams.† The following "line of conduct" is that frequently observable in comets:—They make their first appearance as faint and slow-moving objects, with little or no tail, but by degrees accelerate, enlarge and throw out from them this appendage, which increases in length and brightness till they perform their rapid sweep round the Sun, and are for a while invisible to us.‡ After a brief interval we see them again on the other side of that luminary, and, strange to say, the enormous tail points in the opposite direction, actually preceding the comet in its course.

* Mann's 'Guide to the Knowledge of the Heavens,' p. 229.
† Herschel's 'Treatise,' p. 311.
‡ Comets are not always invisible to us at the time of their perihelion passage. When the plane of a comet's orbit bears some resemblance to that of the earth, the comet will at that time be probably placed so much in the same direction with the sun, as to continue for a while invisible. When, however, its orbit is very much inclined to that of the earth, its perihelion passage may be viewed (so to express it) *in ground plan* instead of *in section*, and a considerable apparent distance may intervene between it and the sun, that is, supposing its orbit to be of such a nature that its *real* approach to that luminary is not very close. For instance, Donati's Comet as it appeared within nine hours after its perihelion passage was several degrees above the horizon, while the sun had set an hour and a half previously.

And now the comet shines with increased splendour (that is, after passing the Sun), the tail increases in real dimensions, and the comet moves with great speed. This velocity gradually diminishes, and ere long the tail of the comet begins to shorten, and eventually dies away, or is absorbed into the head, which itself gradually dwindles down until it is at length altogether lost to our sight.* The disappearance of comets is considered by astronomers to be tolerably well accounted for by supposing them (like the planets) to shine by the reflected light of the Sun.

We shall close this notice of comets by a short account of a few which have appeared during the present century.

First, the comet of 1811. This beautiful object remained for several months in view, giving ample opportunities for the investigation of its movements. It was discovered by Flauguergues, in March, 1811, became a most brilliant object during the ensuing autumn, and was last perceived by a Russian astronomer, in August, 1812.† Its period has, as we have already mentioned, been estimated at upwards of three thousand years. The length of its tail was thirty-six millions of miles, and its greatest apparent length was twenty-five degrees.

Second, the comet of 1835. This was Halley's Comet. It was first detected at Rome, at the Observatory, on August 5th, 1835, and it continued visible till the end of March, 1836, with the exception of a few

* Herschel's 'Treatise,' p. 305.
† Johnson's 'School Atlas of Astronomy,' p. 12.

days in November, during which it performed its passage nearest to the Sun. On account of its southern position after this period, it was not favorably situated for observation in Europe on its re-appearance; but was seen to great advantage at the Cape of Good Hope by Mr. Maclear and Sir John Herschel.* It was of no very remarkable dimensions, though far more visible than it had appeared in 1759. In former centuries its size and brightness had created considerable terror among the superstitious, and when seen by Halley, in 1682, it rivalled the planet Jupiter in brilliancy. On its approach to the Sun in October, 1835, its nucleus and head, as well as its tail, underwent many singular changes of appearance, which, though of a feeble nature compared to those of the remarkable comet of Donati, were diligently watched by astronomers.†

Third, the great comet of 1843. This was an extraordinary object, and seen to most advantage in southern countries. It performed its passage round the Sun on February 27th, and on the following day was visible in broad daylight from various parts of the world. It was seen from the United States, Mexico, Italy, and also, it is said, from the East Indies. On that day the nucleus and tail put together, measured about one degree in length. Its light was equal to that of the Moon on a clear night; and some of the observers compared it to a small cloud strongly illuminated by the Sun.‡ It was seen from Pernambuco, in Brazil, and from Van Die-

---

* Grant's 'History of Physical Astronomy,' p. 138.
† Bond's 'Account of the Comet of Donati,' p. 112.
‡ Loomis's 'Recent Progress of Astronomy,' p. 122.

man's Land, on March 1st. The tail grew rapidly, and, as Bessel remarked, apparently at the expense of the head, as no nucleus seems to have been visible to the naked eye after the first days of March.* About March 5th the tail had reached its greatest length, and stretched to the wonderful extent of sixty-nine degrees. This comet disappeared from view before the middle of April. It was remarkable in the two following particulars:—Firstly its wonderfully near approach to the Sun, for it came to about one-tenth of the Sun's diameter from that luminary! Secondly, the enormous (real) length of its tail, being equal to that of any comet hitherto observed.†

This comet appears, notwithstanding the phenomenon of 1858, *still* to justify Sir John Herschel's description of it, as " by far the most remarkable which has been seen during the present century." All descriptions agree in representing it as a stupendous spectacle,‡ and Mr. Maclear, who has seen Donati's Comet, and remembers the comet of 1811, considers neither of these phenomena as " comparable in splendour to the great comet of 1843."§

Fourth, the comet of 1853. It was discovered with the assistance of the telescope at Gottingen on June 10th, became faintly visible to the naked eye about the 7th of August, and rapidly increased in brilliancy during that month, till, on the 30th, it was as bright as

* Loomis's 'Recent Progress of Astronomy,' p. 126.
† Ibid., p. 131.
‡ 'Outlines of Astronomy,' § 589 (1849).
§ Royal Astronomical Society's 'Monthly Notices,' January, 1859.

one of the brightest stars of the first magnitude. Its effect was, however, much lessened by the nearness to the direction then occupied by the Sun, as the twilight glow overpowered much of its splendour. It travelled southward, and is not known to have been seen from any place in the northern hemisphere after the 4th of September. Its brilliancy diminished after the 15th of that month, but it could be detected from the Cape of Good Hope Observatory up to January 11th, 1854.*

Fifth, the comet of 1854. This comet was remarkable for the short duration of the time in which it was visible. It was discovered as a large and conspicuous object on March 29th, but became almost invisible, even in a powerful telescope, a fortnight later.† Its brilliancy was much overpowered by the presence of moonlight. Mr. Hind calculates the real length of its tail at six millions of miles.

The great comet of 1858 *(Donati's).* Whatever we may surmise respecting the probability of our readers having witnessed the other phenomena portrayed or described in this little work, we may fairly suppose that all who read these pages have seen the great comet of 1858, the *unexpected* appearance of which was, in the words of a popular almanack,‡ a very good substitute for that of the great *expected* comet of 1556. They will probably remember the circumstances attending their first sight of it. A few may have been aware of

* Loomis's 'Recent Progress of Astronomy,' p. 158.
† Breen's 'Planetary Worlds,' p. 265.
‡ 'Illustrated London Almanack' for 1859.

its existence so long ago as June, 1858, on the second evening of which month it was discovered by Dr. G. B. Donati, astronomer at the Museum at Florence, in Right Ascension one hundred and forty degrees eighteen minutes, and North Declination twenty-three degrees forty-seven minutes, close to the position of the star λ in Leo.*

Far greater will be the number to whom the fact of its existence became suddenly known when it appeared after a week of cloudy weather on the calm moonlight evening of Saturday, September 18th. And some of our readers may, like ourselves, have followed the plan indicated at page 21, and having discovered the comet "humbly in the newspaper," where it was described as being visible to the naked eye, and about as conspicuous as a star of the fourth magnitude, having marked on a map its bearings with respect to the principal stars of Ursa Major, and when *they* became visible, have watched

---

* Mr. Hind's Letter to the 'Times,' October 16th, 1858. The comet was discovered independently of Donati's announcement, by Mr. Parkhurst, in the United States. It may interest the reader to be informed that no less than *four* comets were discovered in the year 1858, though but one was visible to the naked eye. The first on March 8th, at Bonne, by Dr. Winnecke; the second on May 2nd, at Cambridge, in the United States, by Mr. Tuttle; the third on May 21st, at Berlin, by Dr. Bruhn; and the fourth on June 2nd, by Donati, at Florence. The periodic comets of Encke and Faye also re-appeared on August 7th and September 8th.

We derive this information, as well as the most interesting facts in connection with Donati's Comet, and some recent particulars about the planets, from the 'Monthly Notices' of the Astronomical Society, which have been most kindly forwarded to us by Sir William R. Hamilton, to whom we wish in this place to record our thanks.

for the comet in the deepening twilight, till they saw it near the Great Bear's left hind foot like a faint star with a short train of light, and which we described in the diary which we thenceforward kept concerning it, as not being so conspicuous as our recollection of the comet of 1854. We little guessed how wonderful an object it was to become.

It had then, however, been known three months to the astronomical world, *but no longer;* for it was not a predicted comet, or one of which astronomers had any previous knowledge. At the time of its discovery it was an excessively faint object, even in the largest telescopes, and moved very slowly; and it was not till the middle of August or later that its future track could be calculated with any degree of correctness.* Its discoverer stated, however, so early as the 27th of June, that he believed the comet would be visible to the naked eye at the time of its perihelion passage.† *How* visible he probably scarcely anticipated.

"When Donati, keeping watch at Florence, discovered in the sky a scarcely perceptible telescopic glimmer, he could have no suspicion of the great splendour and the great renown which his modest nebulosity was shortly to attain. It has now taken rank amongst the most splendid of the wandering stars which European and Chinese history have registered on their annals."‡

When we next saw the comet on the evening of

* Mr. Hind's Letter to the 'Times,' October 16th, 1858.
† 'The Great Comet of 1858: its History and Telescopic Appearance,' published by Hardwicke.
‡ 'Household Words,' October 30th, 1858.

September 12th, it had visibly increased in apparent size, and though not brighter (except quite near the nucleus) than the cloudy spot Præsepe in Cancer, was an unmistakable *comet*, and its tail observed the direction usual with those bodies, namely, pointing away from the Sun. Next morning from half-past three till near sunrise it was a beautiful object in the north-eastern heavens. Cloudy weather concealed it from view till the evening of the 18th, when, as we have already narrated, it was clearly to be seen notwithstanding bright moonlight. Next morning, however, and again on the morning of the 20th, it appeared to far greater advantage, and, as on the 13th, could be watched till near sunrise. It was now certainly brighter than Præsepe, and its nucleus when viewed through the telescope was small and brilliant, appearing about the size of the planet Mars (when at its smallest), but indistinct at the edges.

The comet, still stretching *away* from the Sun, appeared each morning in a different "attitude" from what it had presented in the evening. It had not *really* turned itself, but had merely been *apparently* carried with the whole celestial sphere by our Earth's actual motion on its axis; but these changes of position, coupled with the great difference of brightness caused by the presence or absence of moonlight, gave rise at the time to a popular error, namely, that the morning and the evening comet were two different bodies.

The Chinese could have corrected such a notion more than a thousand years ago. In describing a comet which appeared in 837 they write, "In general when a comet (literally a *broom*) appears in the morning, the tail extends towards the west, when it appears in the evening, towards the east. This is a constant rule."*

On the morning of the 20th, we noted that the comet extended in clearly visible length to a distance similar to that which separates the well-known stars Castor and Pollux. Its nucleus remained in sight till, along with the brightest stars and planets, as Sirius, Procyon, Jupiter, and Saturn, it faded away in the glow of sunrise.

The comet's tail when first observed was straight, but on the morning of the 19th a slight curvature was perceptible; this form, which afterwards became so striking a characteristic of this comet, has also been observed in the case of other large comets.

In a few days moonlight began to interfere with morning observations of the comet; but to make up for this the evening observations improved, owing to the increasing lateness of the hour at which the moon rose: on the evening of the 22nd the curved form of the comet was apparent, and this, with the great brightness of the nucleus, caused it strongly to resemble those fireworks called "serpents." On the 28th our diary pronounces it, in spite of passing clouds, to have been "beyond comparison grander" than we had yet seen

---

* Grant's 'History of Physical Astronomy,' p. 297. The 'Chinese Annals,' in which the above passage occurs, contains notices of comets visible from 613 B.C.; these have been carefully sought out and noted by the late M. Edouard Biot.

it, and extending to a distance corresponding to that which separates Arcturus from Mirach. The nucleus was very bright, and glittered in the telescope more like a star than a planet. It was surrounded by a bright light, very white, and "bean-shaped" rather than round. The rest of the comet was a paler white, but standing out well against the dark sky, especially at its west or "preceding" margin. Again on the 29th was the comet visible, wonderfully increased in length, and having changed its place among the stars with striking rapidity during the past week. But on the next day it appeared in its glory. On the morning of the 30th of September, at a few minutes after eleven, it arrived at its least distance from the Sun.* "At that time," says Mr. Hind, "its distance from the Sun was fifty-five millions of miles, and its rate of moving one hundred and twenty-seven thousand miles per hour." Reader, do we trace a slightly incredulous expression in your countenance, as you read these statistics, so confidentially given? We cannot now enter into any demonstration of their truth, but shall merely say that this comet in its subsequent journey, strikingly verified the mathematical theory of its motion. Its passage across Arcturus on October 5th punctually fulfilled the predictions of astronomers. But to return to September 30th. The appearance of the comet on that cloudless evening suggested the shape of a bird of paradise feather, and was beyond imagination graceful and beautiful. Two small stars shone with undimmed lustre through the delicately transparent

* Mr. Hind's Letter to the 'Times,' October 16th, 1858.

tail. *It never appeared brighter than on that evening;* though its length and breadth subsequently increased to a remarkable degree. Again we saw it on the 3rd and 4th, and on the latter day, the small two-inch telescope revealed a change in the form of the nucleus, or rather of the surrounding light, which now appeared of a semicircular form rather than bean-shaped, and encircled the sides and lower part of the nucleus, while the upper part of the latter stood out sharply against a dark cleft in the centre of the comet's tail. The same appearance was observed on the following evening, and on subsequent occasions. To observers who possessed telescopes of greater power many wonderful changes in the nucleus were visible from night to night. We shall presently revert to these; and, meanwhile, continue our description of its appearance as noted by ourselves.

The weather on October 5th must have been anxiously watched by thousands who were aware that on that evening this comet was to pass between us and Arcturus, the brightest star north of the Equinoctial.

A calm lovely afternoon was followed by a tranquil sunset; and scarcely had the twilight begun when Arcturus could be descried, small, bright, and yellow, closely accompanied by a far fainter spot, perfectly white. This was the comet; we have described it as "perfectly white at that time (the colour of the Moon by day), and with scarcely any brightness; its appearance was rather like wool or cotton." The nucleus showed well against the dark cleft, as on the preceding night. By half-past six much more of the tail appeared, and the comet began to pass over Arcturus; at seven the star shone with great brightness through the comet's tail, and at half-past seven appeared to the east of it.

This transit of the comet across Arcturus was, in Professor Nichol's words, " a spectacle, the like of which no one might see again, although he should spend on earth some fifty lives."* The part of the comet which passed in front of Arcturus was but a short distance from the head, and was of more dense composition than the remoter portions of the tail. On that memorable evening Professor Nichol observed several small telescopic stars shining brightly through a part of the tail still "denser than that which endeavoured to eclipse Arcturus." At the very utmost it absorbed one-fourth of their light. Our atmosphere— pure transparent air—is proved to absorb one-fourth of a star's light; that is to say, the stars appear to us only three-fourths as bright as they would do if no atmosphere intervened. But the comet's tail was at least a thousand times deeper than our atmosphere, for the thickness of our atmosphere is only about forty miles, whereas the comet's diameter at its narrowest part was upwards of twenty thousand miles, and upwards of sixty thousand at the part which crossed Arcturus. How amazingly small must have been its density!*

The following woodcut will give a sufficient idea of the average appearance of the comet from October 2nd

---

* "Donati's Comet," by Professor Nichol, in the Scottish Annual' for 1859.

to 11th. We have particularly noted its increasing transparency and *harmlessness* of appearance. "Though

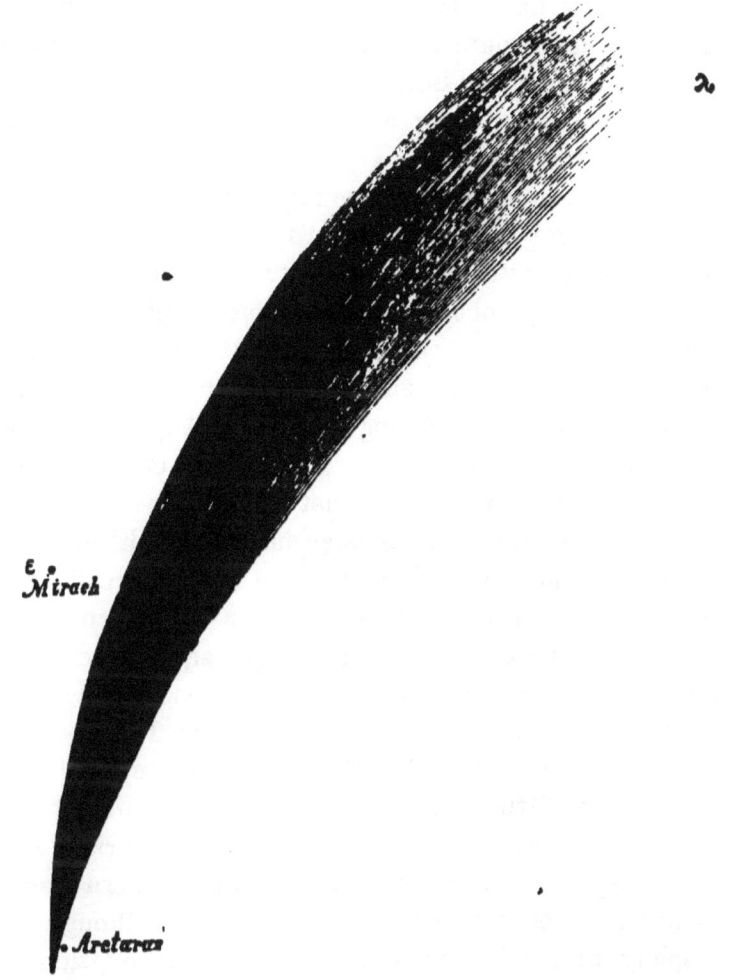

very visible and remarkable," says our diary, "it is so graceful, so feathery and filmy, that it scarcely seems capable of inspiring dread." On one evening we recorded an irregularity in its outline on the convex side, as though it curved slightly backward; and similar appearances have also been alluded to by observers in England and America. "Altogether," says the 'Report of the Astronomical Society's Council,' "its appearance was like that of a large ostrich feather when waved gently in the hand."

As the comet travelled south its head each evening pointed more and more inward, in the observance of the usual comet rule of the tail turning away from the Sun.* On October 11th, the comet appeared as in Plate IX. It was " very long and also broad, covering a great area of the heavens, but, except near the nucleus, faint and filmy, resembling the Milky Way, which was conspicuous this evening. The *breadth* of the Milky Way also gives an idea of that of the comet." " We viewed this wonderful mysterious tail with unbated curiosity and admiration, and we saw it no more! Cloudy weather followed, and when a clear evening at last came (October 16th) moonlight again interfered, and the comet scarcely appeared as conspicuous as it had done on the evening of September 18th, but on October 16th it pointed in the contrary direction, being now south of the Sun. The next clear evening it was gone,—concealed by a bank of fog at the horizon and by twilight,—gone to the skies of the southern hemisphere, to be visible till after January, though in rapidly decreasing splendour, and the temptation to

* See foregoing illustration.

cross the Line and follow it must have been great with hearty astronomers."*

So much for our private observations of the comet of Donati. We now take up the narrative as told from this point by others. For a few days later than the 16th, it remained in the view of observers whose accurately-adjusted instruments enabled them to discover it in the day-time. On the 18th, it passed near the real position of the planet Venus, that is, according to Dr. Nichol, within about nine millions of miles from it, so that it must have been attracted by the planet, "to a certain extent, from its course, and compelled to move in a different ellipse from that in which it has previously gone. Such contingencies, however, could in the case of Donati's Comet be calculated for with some degree of accuracy, as the recent celestial visitor appeared under circumstances more than usually favorable for observation."†

The comet appears to have been last seen from European observatories about the 22nd of October.‡ Before that day, however, it had come into view in southern latitudes. Mr. Maclear, of the Cape of Good Hope Observatory, caught sight of it on October 11th, and from that day to December 14th, was able to observe it fifty-three times.§ On the 7th of October it was seen simultaneously by observers at Loando, on the west coast of Africa, and at Rio Janeiro and Buenos

* 'Household Words,' October 30th, 1858.
† Professor Nichol's Lecture "On Comets," reported in the 'North British Daily Mail,' November 9th, 1858.
‡ Royal Astronomical Society's 'Monthly Notices,' February, 1869.
§ Ibid., January, 1859, p. 92.

Ayres.* On the very same day it came in sight a Lyttelton, New Zealand,† and on October 11th, wa‥ first seen from Melbourne, in Australia.‡ At the two latter places it came unannounced, having travelled more quickly than the news of its appearance in the skies of the "old country;" so that the observer at Melbourne described it merely as "*a* large comet," while the New Zealand journalist made sure of its being the predicted and long-expected phenomenon of 1556.

Donati's Comet strikingly exemplified the phenomena observed in many of these mysterious bodies, of particles streaming with great force from the nucleus towards the Sun, and then turning back again away from the Sun to form the tail.

Perhaps even in our days, the nature of that mysterious force which acts upon comets will be discovered. If so, the discoverer will indeed (to imitate the well-known words of Newton) have rescued a precious gem from the vast ocean of still unexplored Truth!

Donati's Comet will long continue a theme of interest in the minds of astronomers. Nor should the subject of comets be too readily dismissed from the minds of the "general public," who perchance pay more attention to them as splendid and extraordinary objects than as topics of philosophical inquiry.

* Royal Astronomical Society's 'Monthly Notices,' December, 1858, p. 67.
† 'Lyttelton Times,' October 11th.
‡ 'Athenæum,' January 15th, 1859.

CHAPTER XI.

SHOOTING STARS AND OTHER LUMINOUS METEORS.

ON a clear night, while the observer is engaged in examining the planets and stars, his attention is occasionally arrested by certain luminous appearances in the sky. As this little work undertakes to give an account of any commonly observable phenomena, we will briefly allude to some of these appearances.

Passing by the *ignis fatuus* and the lunar halos, which, with the bright rainbow seen by day, and also the phenomena of lightning, are pretty well accounted for, as belonging to this earth and its atmosphere, we pause to ask questions of the Aurora Borealis, and the corresponding appearance in the far regions of the southern hemisphere; and also of the shooting stars, which every observer, who spends any length of time out of doors on a favorable night, will be sure to see occasionally. (Plate X.)

As to the Aurora, its nature is as yet only conjectured, but it is proved to be in some way influenced by magnetism. The subject has been much studied; and many observations have been recorded; but still this imposing phenomenon, in its varying aspects—its spreading rays occasionally reaching the zenith with a peculiar undulating motion, occasionally darting from side to side, as some relate, like javelins hurled by contending parties—is very little understood. There is as yet no theory of the Aurora; we must still (in Dr. Nichol's words) "*observe* and *wait*."*

A similar mystery pervades the subject of the falling or shooting stars. Here again we are informed that Science has "a vast deal to learn from prolonged and assiduous observation." Yet much has been observed, and many interesting facts have been proved respecting these meteors. We proceed to state the most remarkable of these.

The shooting stars, though incomparably nearer than the *fixed* stars among which they appear, are yet at a very considerable distance. The proof of this is, that the same shooting star has often been simultaneously observed by two spectators widely separated from each other. In fact, the best mode of observing them with a view to ascertaining their real heights, is by two or more persons systematically arranging to look out for any which might appear, and carefully to note the direction in which any such shooting star was seen; and by combining the measure thus obtained, to deduce its real place.

Shooting stars, observed in this way, have been proved to appear at heights varying from four to eighty miles; and it is stated that some have come into view

* Nichol's 'Cyclopædia,' p. 55.

Shooting Stars and other Luminous Meteors. 117

at the wonderful altitude of two hundred and forty-eight miles above the earth.*

A second remakable feature about them is, their great velocity. This has been stated at from eighteen to thirty-six miles in a *second;* while the motion of the Earth in its orbit is under seventeen miles in the same space of time.†

This wonderful rapidity of movement seems to suggest that the shooting stars are really *from afar,* and notwithstanding their small size are of a *planetary* nature. There is another very extraordinary fact in connection with them, which also points to the same conjecture. It has been observed that in various years the night of the 12th of November has been remarkable for the immense numbers of these meteors, which have been observable. They do not invariably appear at this period, but have done so on a great many occasions. There is also a periodical fall of them in August, about the 10th day of that month.

The theory proposed to account for these periodical visits of the shooting stars, is that a belt of them—situated somewhere within the limits of the Solar System—revolves round the Sun, and cuts through that portion of the Earth's orbit which our planet must occupy on those particular nights in August and November.

The falling stars of November 12th, 1833, were seen in great brilliancy from the United States of America; the following particulars concerning them are from a

* 'Cosmos,' vol. iii, p. 434.
† Ibid., p. 435.

New York newspaper:*—"Some time before twelve o'clock [at night], the meteors so frequently seen on summer evenings, called shooting stars, were observed to fall with unusual frequency and splendour. They continued from that hour to flash across the skies more and more until they were eclipsed by the glories of the rising sun this morning." "Were it possible to enumerate them in the swiftness of their arrowy haste, we might venture to say that for the space of two hours, intervening between four and six, more than a thousand per minute might have been counted."

"In one instance we distinctly heard the explosion of a meteor, that shot across to the north-west, leaving a broad and luminous track; and witnessed another, which left a path of light that was clearly discernible for more than ten minutes after the ball, if such it be, had exploded."

What were these last-mentioned meteors? They take us to another, perhaps a widely different branch of the subject. Beside the shooting stars, there are luminous meteors, called "fire-balls," sometimes observed in connection with those truly strange visitants, the "Meteoric Stones or Aërolites."

The existence of meteoric stones, that is to say, the statement that mineral substances of considerable weight had actually fallen on the earth through the atmosphere, was long disregarded as a mere fiction unworthy of belief. But on April 26th, 1803, a number of stones fell in broad daylight from a small

* 'The New York Commercial Advertiser,' November 13th, 1833; quoted in Middleton's 'Celestial Atlas.'

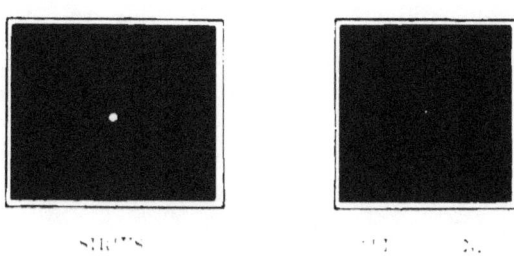

SIRIUS.

MIZAR ALCOR.

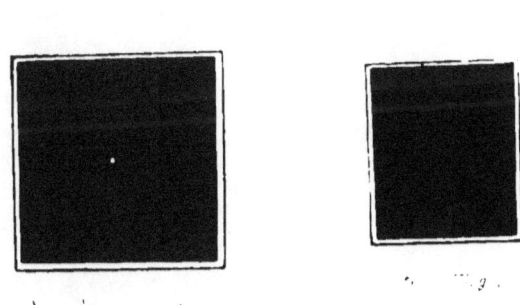

seconds must be. The expressions "angle of a degree" or of ten degrees, or minutes, or seconds, are all used to describe the inclination of two lines to each other.

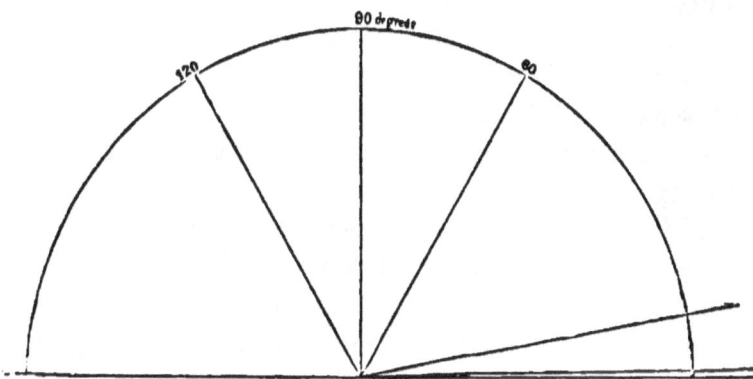

From this diagram may be seen the inclination of angles of one hundred and twenty degrees, of ninety, sixty, and ten degrees, and of a single degree. This latter, it will be observed is a very small angle; its two sides are not very unlike parallel lines. An angle of a *minute* is only *one-sixtieth part* of this.

If we draw a circle ten feet across, then *one degree* on its circumference will measure about an inch. If we draw a circle six hundred feet across, then *one minute* on its circumference will measure about an inch; and a degree will be about five feet.

Or what comes to the same thing, if we set up something about an inch in diameter, and view it at the distance of five feet, lines drawn from it to our eyes will make an angle of a degree. The same object viewed at the distance of three hundred feet will make an angle of *a minute* with our eyes.

But a *second* is a much smaller thing; it is but *one-sixtieth of a minute—one three thousand six hundredth of a degree.* An angle of a second is that at which an object of about an inch in diameter would be seen at the distance of *three miles.* Such an object could only be seen with the aid of a telescope; yet there are instruments constructed capable of measuring so small an angle.

If (to reverse the experiments above suggested) we draw a line about five feet long on the ground, and ascertain that lines drawn from some distant point to each end of this line would make an angle of a degree, we should know that the distant point was three hundred feet away, without going from our *base line* to measure the three hundred feet.

If it were possible to employ a longer base line than five feet, it would make the measurement rather easier, and no surveyor would employ so small a base.

As has been seen, the base line used in measuring the distance of the Sun, was the Earth's diameter, nearly eight thousand miles. But this base line is of no use whatever in measuring the distance of the *stars.* Lines drawn to a star from the most distant points of the Earth have absolutely no appreciable inclination to each other. The most delicately-constructed instruments cannot detect the smallest fraction of the angle of a second. The diameter of the Earth is an utterly insufficient base line.*

* Arago's 'Lectures,' p. 17.

Fixed Stars.

But it is in the power of astronomers to employ a far larger base line. The Earth, by its annual motion round the Sun, changes its position in space to the extent of one hundred and ninety millions of miles every six months. Now it is practicable to ascertain the direction of a star as seen from these two opposite points of the Earth's orbit. This experiment has been tried; for instance, Hook, Flamstead, and Bradley, eminent astronomers of the last two centuries, observed a star in the constellation Draco, expecting that the diameter of the Earth's orbit would form an angle with it.

The surprising result was that there was no angle whatever, capable of being detected.* This great space, one hundred and ninety millions of miles, did not bear so large a proportion to the distance of a star, as *one inch* does to *three miles*.

In later years the great accuracy with which instruments are made, and the persevering efforts which have been directed to the subject, have enabled astronomers to detect very slight angles, or, as they are called, "parallaxes" of some of the fixed stars. But these are all under a second, except in the case of one star, of which the parallax is believed to be two seconds.†

So immensely distant from us, and probably no less so from each other,* and shining so brightly, what are they? In all probability *suns* like ours, and many of them superior to it in size, and, perhaps, giving light

---

* Arago's ' Lectures,' p. 17.
† Airy's ' Lectures,' p. 172.

to groups of surrounding planets. The larger ones are probably the nearest to us. It is, however, believed that the nearest of all in the northern hemisphere is a comparatively small star.*

As we look at these stars, and vainly try to realize their vast distance, a startling thought may occur to us —how long has their light taken to come here? And if the stars were to be *destroyed*, how long would their light continue to reach us with undiminished brilliancy? If a star can be ascertained to have a parallax of *one second*, its light would take *three years* to reach this Earth.† That star might have been quenched a year ago, and would yet continue to shine on us for two years to come! But if one of the *nearest* stars is thus far away, how distant must be those thousand and ten thousand stars that the telescope alone reveals! and every increase of telescopic power brings new stars into view.

Having contemplated the starry firmament as a whole, let us now single out from among its glittering gems some few which bear an individual character of their own. Next to the striking difference in their magnitudes, the marked variety of colour in some of them will catch the eye. Some are reddish, some bright yellow, others lucid white. The unassisted eye will not, however, easily perceive any further peculiarities among the starry host; nor would the observer readily suspect with how keen an interest certain of their number are regarded by the astronomical world.

* 'Cosmos,' vol. iii, p. 190.
† Herschel's 'Treatise,' p. 378.

We shall presently advert to these; and first point out to our readers the remarkable stars, Arcturus, Sirius, and Aldebaran, interesting for the difference of their colours, and also as being among the number of stars which have been observed by mankind from the most remote antiquity.

ARCTURUS.

The bright star in the constellation Bootes was called by the Greek astronomers Arcturus, from its being near the tail of the "Great Bear," Arctos. The term "Arctic Regions" is also derived from this constellation.* Arcturus is a bright star, of a golden colour. It will be remembered that its name occurs twice in the book of Job:—"Which maketh Arcturus, Orion, and Pleiades, and the chambers of the south;" (probably the southern constellations,) and "Canst thou guide Arcturus with his sons?"—Job ix, 9, and xxxviii, 32. The Hebrew word is "Hash," but it does not appear certain whether the star meant was Arcturus or not.†

The parallax of Arcturus is calculated at less than thirteen hundredths (less than one-eighth) of a second.‡

SIRIUS.

Sirius, according to Sir John Herschel, is the

* Chambers' 'Dictionary' (1787).
† Brown's 'Dictionary of the Bible,'
‡ 'Cosmos,' vol. iii, p. 190.

brightest of all the fixed stars.* Yet, compared to the Sun, it gives us very little light. Sir John Herschel, calculating from some experiments by Dr. Wollaston on the light of Sirius, says that the Sun, "in order that it should appear to us no brighter than Sirius, would require to be removed to one hundred and forty-one thousand four hundred times its actual distance."

But it is believed that Sirius is very much farther away than this; it would appear that it is not the nearest fixed star, and that in point of size and intrinsic splendour, it "is in all probability vastly greater than our Sun."† The light of Sirius is perfectly white. Yet various ancient writers have described it as *red*, and have classed it among the decidedly reddish stars of the firmament. It would seem as if some great revolution had taken place, probably in its luminous atmosphere.

"It offers the solitary example of an historically proved alteration of colour" in a star.‡

ALDEBARAN.

This star is the largest in the constellation Taurus, and is often called "The Bull's Eye."§ The Arabian astronomers gave it the name of Aldebaran. It is of a reddish hue.

* Herschel's 'Treatise,' p. 379.
† Ibid., p. 380.
‡ 'Cosmos,' vol. iii, p. 112.
§ Middleton's 'Celestial Atlas,' p. 25.

The observer will soon perceive by consulting the map or globe, that the limits of the various magnitudes are by no means easily ascertained. Bright stars of the second magnitude will be found equal in splendour to many of the first, and the magnitudes are differently set down in different maps. The total number of first magnitude stars, however, southern as well as northern, is generally estimated nearly alike. Humboldt (on Argelander's authority) gives the number of these as twenty;* Sir John Herschel as twenty-three or twenty-four;† the second magnitude Herschel states to contain fifty or sixty, and the third about two hundred; and the number increases very rapidly as we descend in the scale of brightness.† The stars already registered by the care and perseverance of astronomers, down to the seventh magnitude inclusive, amount to from twelve thousand to fifteen thousand.† Of these, the number visible to the unassisted eye throughout the entire heavens—that is, by an observer who should have opportunities of successively scanning both the northern and southern hemisphere in every part—is stated at from five thousand to five thousand eight hundred.‡

Among this great number of sparkling points, long believed by the ancient philosophers to be unchangeable,§ the vigilant eyes of astronomers have detected a few which are subject to periodical variations in the intensity of their lustre; that is to say, there are a few

* 'Cosmos,' vol. iii, p. 89.
† 'Outlines of Astronomy,' § 779.
‡ 'Cosmos,' vol. iii, p. 89.
§ Grant's 'History of Physical Astronomy,' p. 538.

stars in the heavens which, after shining with equal light during a number of days or hours, are observed to diminish in lustre, in some cases becoming invisible to the naked eye; after which they gradually revive. This diminution and increase are accomplished in periods of more or less regularity. M. Argelander reckons the number of variable stars with satisfactorily determined periods as only twenty-four;* but there are many others in which a variation of lustre has been observed without any certainty having yet been attained about the times of its fluctuations.

The most celebrated of the periodically variable stars is that marked *o* (Omicron) in Cetus, the Whale, and from its singular changes called Mira, or the wonderful star.

It remains at its greatest brightness about a fortnight, being then on some occasions equal to a large star of the second magnitude, decreases during about three months, till it becomes completely invisible to the naked

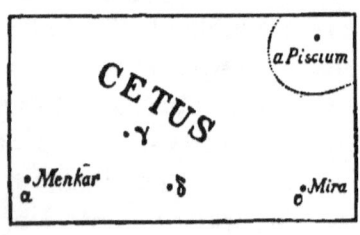

eye; and in that state it remains about five months. It then increases, till at the completion of the period of three hundred and thirty-one days, fifteen hours, and seven minutes, it has regained its first brightness. Such is the general course of its phases.† It does not,

---

* 'Cosmos,' vol. iii, p. 161.

† Ibid., pp. 161, 163, and 'Outlines of Astronomy,' § 820.

however, always return to exactly the same degree of brightness, or increase or diminish by the same gradations. Nor are the intervals of its greatest brilliancy always exactly equal, though the above period of three hundred and thirty-one days, etc., indicates the average interval, as calculated during a great number of years.

The variable brightness of Mira has been known since 1596.* Its period was discovered by Holwarda, in the year 1639;† and from that time to the year 1851, two hundred and seventy-nine of its wonderful fluctuations have been observed. It can be conveniently compared with the principal stars of Cetus. It usually attains a brilliancy equal to that of the star γ;‡ but at its maximum in October, 1839, it exceeded Menkar, the brightest star in Cetus;* and in November, 1779, it was only a little inferior to Aldebaran;§ while at some other times of maximum brightness, it has not even attained the lustre of δ Ceti, which is only of the fourth magnitude.§ Possibly these apparent irregularities may themselves be found on further observation to recur at stated intervals.||

Having given a detailed account of Omicron Ceti, as a striking example of this wonderful and mysterious class of objects, we annex a sort of table¶ of five other remarkable periodical stars, which the reader may identify in the actual heavens. The relative degrees of

* 'Outlines of Astronomy,' § 820.
† 'Cosmos,' vol. iii, p. 161.
‡ Ibid., p. 164.   § Ibid., p. 157. || Ibid., p. 156.
¶ From the Table of Variable Stars, sent to Humboldt by M. Argelander, of Bonn Observatory. See 'Cosmos,' vol. iii, p. 161.

brightness with which they are represented in the annexed figures, are those with which they appeared on the evening of November, 12th, 1858; except in the case of Beta Lyræ; that star is shown as observed on December 3rd :—

ALGOL OR β (BETA) PERSEI.

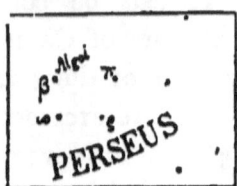

Maximum, two and three-tenths magnitude; minimum, four magnitude; period, two days, twenty hours, forty-nine minutes; date of discovery, 1669, by Montanari, as subject to variations of brightness. Its period ascertained in 1782, by Goodricke.

χ (CHI) CYGNI.

Maximum, six and seven-tenths to four magnitude; minimum, invisible; period, four hundred and six days, one hour, thirty minutes; date of discovery, 1687, by Kirch.

It is generally visible during only fifty-two days out of the four hundred and six, and seldom brighter at its maximum than the fifth magnitude. A hundred and forty-five periods of χ Cygni had been observed up to 1851.

β (BETA) LYRÆ.

Maximum, three and four-tenths magnitude; minimum, four and five-tenths magnitude; period, twelve days, twenty-one hours, forty-five minutes; date of discovery, 1784, by Goodricke.

The discoverer at first calculated its period at six days and nine hours, but after continuing his observations for some time, he found that at each *alternate* time of least brightness, it diminished to the faintness of stars between the 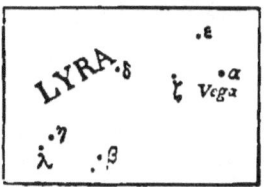 fourth and fifth magnitude; while at the intermediate "minima" its lustre sank only to between the third and fourth magnitude. Therefore it followed that the *whole* course of its phases occupied nearly thirteen days, its period in reality comprising two maxima and two minima. From seventeen hundred to eighteen hundred periods of β Lyræ had been observed up to 1851.*

η (NU) AQUILÆ, OTHERWISE CALLED
η ANTINOI.

Maximum, three and four-tenths magnitude; minumum, five and four-tenths magnitude; period, seven days, four hours, fourteen minutes; date of discovery, 1784, by E. Pigott.

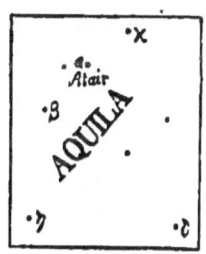

* 'Cosmos,' vol. iii, p. 168.

At its maximum it is brighter than η Aquilæ, but does not equal δ.*

δ (DELTA) CEPHEI.

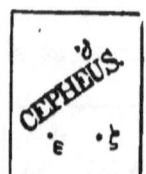

Maximum, four and three-tenths magnitude; minimum, five and four-tenths magnitude; period, five days, eight hours, forty-nine minutes; date of discovery, 1784, by Goodricke.

This is the most regular in its periods of all known variable stars.†

Several persons have endeavoured to account for the phenomena of periodically variable stars, but no satisfactory view of the subject has been arrived at by any inquirer.‡ It has been suggested that they may revolve round fixed axes, and that a great part of their surfaces may be obscure. Goodricke suggested that Algol might be accompanied by a planet which revolved round it, and occasionally shut away a part of its light from our eyes.§

Additions are slowly made to the list of these wonderful objects. Argelander enumerates thirteen which have been detected since the year 1800;|| but for the most part they are either telescopic stars, or else their changes of brightness are so slight that they cannot

---

* 'Cosmos,' vol. iii, p. 168.
† Ibid., p. 169.
‡ Grant's 'History of Physical Astronomy,' p. 541.
§ Ibid., and 'Outlines of Astronomy,' § 821.
|| 'Cosmos,' vol. iii, p. 161.

easily be observed. There is one star (marked 30 Hydræ in the Catalogue of Hevelius) discovered by Maraldi, in 1704, the period of which is ninety-five days longer than that of χ Cygni.* This is the longest ascertained period, and the shortest is that of Algol. It is not certain whether Mira ever becomes absolutely invisible at its minima; at those periods it has sometimes been seen, of the eleventh or twelfth magnitude, but, of course, only through a telescope.†

The phenomenon of varying brightness is not limited to the stars which we have just been considering; there are also others which, without having shown any signs of periodic changes, have undergone a decided alteration of brilliancy, as attested by trustworthy maps and records. Some stars which have been visible for ages are believed to have entirely disappeared, and the rare spectacle has occasionally been seen of a new star suddenly shining forth with great lustre, and after some months of gradually decreasing splendour, completely fading away.‡

So true it is, that "change" is written even on the majestic lights of the firmament. We now come to quite a different class of phenomena among the stars, singularly interesting, as enabling us (in Sir John Herschel's words) "unhesitatingly to declare them subject to the same dynamical laws, and obedient to the same power of gravitation, which govern our own system."§

* 'Cosmos,' vol. iii, p. 161.   † Ibid., p. 163.
‡ Grant's 'History of Physical Astronomy,' p. 539.
§ 'Outlines of Astronomy,' § 833.

DOUBLE STARS.

Many of the stars, when examined with the telescope, are found to be double, that is, to consist of two or even more stars placed near together.

When we consider the great number of the stars, and their different distances, we can easily imagine that two stars might only *appear* double in the direction from which we see them.* Sir William Herschel observed the double stars with great attention for more than twenty-five years. His reason for observing them was this:

He concluded that where two stars were of very different size, though close together, the smaller one was in reality far behind the other, as one tree in an

open field might appear close to another, to an observer who stood with the nearer tree almost in a straight line between himself and the distant one. By moving

* Herschel's 'Treatise,' p. 385.

Fixed Stars.

a few steps to the right or left, this observer would see the trees appearing to approach, or recede from each other. And by returning to his first position, he would, of course, see them as at first.

Herschel thought that he could ascertain the distances of the stars from the Earth by observing the apparent changes of position in two such stars, as seen from different points of the Earth's path round the Sun.*

He noted down the positions and apparent distances of eight hundred and forty-six double stars,† but he was much surprised at certain phenomena which presented themselves.

He expected that the apparent distances of the two stars of a double star would alternately increase and lessen every six months, as the observer was restored to his first position by the motion of the Earth, or again removed from it.

But instead of this, he observed, in many instances, a regular *progressive* change.* And after long investigating the movements of these stars, he came to the conclusion that many of the double stars did not merely *appear* double, but that the stars which composed them *really belonged to each other*, and that *both revolved round some central point between them.*‡ Their movements may be illustrated by two persons walking round and round a circular table, and always keeping its diameter between them.

---

* Herschel's 'Treatise,' p. 386.
† 'Cosmos,' vol. iii, p. 203.
‡ Herschel's 'Treatise,' p. 389.

This kind of movement Herschel perceived in only some of the many double stars which he examined. To these the name of "binary systems" has been given. But it requires a long course of years to observe the movements of these stars, as their relative changes of place are (in most cases) so slight even in ten years; and therefore many may be *binary* systems which are at present merely classed as double stars.*

In fact, the number of known revolving stars is gradually increasing. In a table published in 1849, six thousand "multiple" stars are enumerated (that is, groups of two, three, or sometimes four stars); and of these, an alteration of relative position has been observed in six hundred and fifty.*

It is a curious fact that when two stars in a binary system are of very unequal size, they are frequently of different colours, the large one being generally reddish or yellow, and the smaller one blue.†

Though these stars each revolve, there is no reason to suppose they are not surrounded, each by a group of planets.†

The times of revolution of some of these stars have been calculated, and appear in some cases to be very long periods. The stars longest in revolving, judging by the rate at which they have moved since first observed, appear to take *five hundred years*.‡ The shortest period of revolution yet ascertained is thirty years.‡

---

* 'Cosmos,' vol. iii, p. 207.
† Herschel's 'Treatise,' p. 395.
‡ 'Cosmos,' vol. iii, p. 214.

Fixed Stars. 139

QUADRUPLE STAR IN LYRA.

ε (Epsilon) in the constellation Lyra, is a very curious quadruple star. It generally appears as a single star to the naked eye, but on a very clear night, persons with good sight may observe it to be double; and a small telescope shows the stars considerably separated from each other.

A powerful telescope exhibits *each of them* as a very minute double star.* All four belong to each other, and form what has been termed a "quaternary system."†

MIZAR AND ALCOR.

The largest star in this drawing is ζ (Zeta) in Ursa Major (or the Great Bear); it is the second star to the left in that constellation, thus—

The Arabian astronomers called it *Mizar*. If observed carefully, a smaller may be seen just above it. This star was named *Alcor* by the Arabians. They also called it "Saidak," or the "tester," as they considered it could only be discerned by persons with very good sight.‡

* Middleton's 'Celestial Atlas,' p. 55.
† 'Cosmos,' vol. iii, p. 211.
‡ Ibid., p. 48.

Our telescope separates these stars widely, and shows that Mizar is double.

CASTOR.

α (Alpha) in the constellation Gemini, generally called *Castor*, is classed among stars of the first magnitude. But when viewed with a telescope, it is found to consist of two stars of between the third and fourth magnitude.*

These stars revolve round each other in a period that has been variously estimated by various astronomers. In 1849, after they had been observed during a long time, Sir John Herschel estimated their period of revolution at two hundred and fifty-two years.†

RAS ALGETHI, or ALPHA HERCULIS.

This double star is in the head of Hercules. Its component parts are red and blue, and placed at the distance of four seconds from each other.‡

ALBIREO, or BETA CYGNI.

Albireo is a beautiful double star; its component

---

* Herschel's 'Treatise,' p. 385.
† 'Cosmos,' vol. iii, p. 214.
‡ 'Outlines of Astronomy,' § 836.

Fixed Stars. 141

parts separated to the distance of forty seconds. It is in the beak of the Swan.*

GAMMA VIRGINIS.

This is one of the most remarkable of the double stars, on account of the rapid alteration of distance between the stars which compose it. It has been known to be a double star since the beginning of the eighteenth century, at which time the distance of the two stars was between six and seven seconds, so that any good telescope would show them separate. Since that time they constantly approached, till the year 1836, when they appeared as one star.†

Their distance is now widening again, and the astronomical eye-piece of a two-inch telescope readily shows the separation between them.

The astronomer Bradley, in 1718, fortunately noted in the margin of one of his observation-books, the apparent direction of their line of junction, as compared with two stars in the constellation Virgo; and this record, lately rescued from oblivion by Rigaud, has proved of signal service in the investigation of their orbit.‡ Their presumed period of revolution, as stated by Hind, is one hundred and seventy-four years.

* Middleton's 'Celestial Atlas.'
† Hind's 'Illustrated London Astronomy.'
‡ Herschel's 'Treatise,' p. 392.

CHAPTER XIII.

CLUSTERS OF STARS AND NEBULÆ.

IN clear weather, when the stars are very distinct, we see in several parts of the celestial sphere whitish spots shedding a faint light.

On examining these with a telescope, we discover in them a multitude of little stars set very close together. The united light of these stars causes the whitish appearance observed.*

In some instances, as in the Pleiades, a few stars may be detected with the naked eye; in others they appear with a very small telescope.

But with a very good telescope, many of these faint spots may be *discovered*, which are too small to be seen with the naked eye; and these, again, may be *"resolved"* into stars (as the expression is) by a telescope of extraordinary power.

From their *cloudy* appearance, these telescopic spots have received the name of "Nebulæ."

THE PLEIADES AND HYADES.

Two conspicuous groups of stars in the constellation Taurus were named by the Greek astronomers, The

---
* Arago's 'Lectures,' p. 15.

Hyades and Pleiades, in honour of the twelve daughters of Atlas, King of Mauritania.*

The Hyades consist of five stars, placed in a figure resembling V. The largest of them is the star Aldebaran.

The Pleiades are often called the Seven Stars, a name by which they have been known for ages. Yet the number generally seen is but *six;* and the story the ancients told was that the seven Pleiades being daughters of a sea-nymph, were changed into a constellation, and that the stars of *Alcyone, Maia, Electra, Tayeta, Sterope,* and *Cœleno* shone brightly, but that *Merope's* star was dim, because in her life-time she had *married a mortal.* Some even said her star had entirely disappeared.*

Galileo early examined the Pleiades with his telescope, and counted no less than forty stars in this cluster.†

PRÆSEPE.

Near the centre of the constellation Cancer is a nebula, called Præsepe. As seen by the naked eye, it looks very like a distant nebula as observed with the telescope.

A telescope of very moderate power resolves it into small stars.‡

* 'Cosmos,' vol. iii, p. 48.
† 'Martyrs of Science,' p. 25.
‡ Herschel's 'Treatise,' p. 398.

THE NEBULA IN ORION.

This very remarkable object was first discovered by Huygens, in 1656.* It is close to the star θ (Theta). In fact the four stars near its centre, appearing to the naked eye as only one, compose the star Theta. With a very superior telescope their number is increased to *six*.†

The nebula is exceedingly large, compared to the generality of those which have been observed.

Sir John Herschel says of it, "It is formed of little flocky masses, like wisps of cloud; and such wisps seem to adhere to many small stars at its outskirts, and especially to one considerable star (represented in the figure below the nebula), which it envelopes with a nebulous atmosphere of considerable extent and irregular figure.

"Several astronomers, on comparing this nebula with the figures of it handed down to us by its discoverer Huygens, have concluded that its form has undergone a perceptible change. But when it is considered how difficult it is to represent such an object duly, and how entirely its appearance will differ, even in the same telescope, according to the clearness of the air, or other temporary causes, we shall readily admit that we have no evidence of change that can be relied on."‡

It might be supposed that this large nebula, so early

---

* 'Cosmos,' vol. iii, p. 221.
† Ibid., p. 211.
‡ Herschel's 'Treatise,' p. 403.

THE PLEIADES, as viewed with a very small telescope. 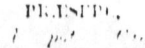PRÆSEPE,

Position of the Hyades and Pleiades.

Clusters of Stars and Nebulæ. 145

discovered, and easily seen through small telescopes, would, when viewed through more powerful instruments, be readily resolved into stars.

Yet when viewed through Herschel's gigantic telescope, it still appeared like a luminous cloud; and very many other nebulæ alike remained unresolved; so that philosophers began to conjecture that this luminous matter was not composed of multitudes of distant stars, but was a kind of half-condensed substance, which would hereafter *harden* into stars.

The nebula in Orion is of a strange, shapeless figure; many of the others, however, appeared in Herschel's telescope of wonderfully regular form, round, ring-shaped, oval, etc., and it was thought that these were *nearly condensed*.

A yet more powerful instrument was required to show that some, at least, of these objects were not masses of *luminous matter*, but each a distant universe, a "heaven of stars."

Such an instrument has been constructed by Lord Rosse. On one of the first nights his six-foot telescope was ever used, a great number of nebulæ, hitherto considered irresolvable, were found to be composed of stars; others presented indications of being resolvable with increased power; and it appears probable that every increase of telescopic power would add to the number of ascertained clusters of stars.

Sir John Herschel published, in 1833, a list of no less than two thousand three hundred and seven nebulæ and clusters, most of which had been discovered by his father. It will, of course, be long before these can all be examined by the *one* telescope which can show them distinctly.

And there is no doubt that during the course of such an examination a great many new and remote nebulæ would appear to this telescope, not resolved, but faintly dawning on our view.

Though the telescope in each successive increase to its power has revealed numerous minute stars, besides those of the nebulæ, the idea is general among astronomers that a powerful telescope might detect the farthest of *these* stars, and show free, clear space beyond, with nothing between them and the still more distant region where the nearest nebula presents itself.*

In fact, that the bright firmament nightly spread over our heads is itself a nebula, an "island world," bounded by that luminous zone called the Milky Way, which is found to be composed of minute stars.*

The suggestive term of an "island world" (used by German writers) is intended to denote the supposition (for as yet it by no means amounts to a certainty) that the stars are not scattered everywhere through Space, but collected into groups. If modern science should prove that no "nebulous matter" exists, and if the Milky Way can indeed be fathomed in every part, then may we say that so much of infinite Space as our greatest telescopes can command, is filled with many thousand isolated groups of stars, separated from each other by intervals so immense, that we can form no adequate conception of them.

In one of these groups stands, as a unit, our Sun,

* Nichol's 'Cyclopædia,' p. 695.

with all its planets and comets, large and small. It is wonderful that man, a creature of a day, can soar so far as to speculate thus on the position of his dwelling-place. And yet how little is revealed to us, compared to the great, the boundless sum of what remains unknown! "What we know," said a dying philosopher, "is but a little matter; what we do not know is immense."*

Who shall say what wonders of creation may be contained in those distant worlds? what amazing scenes of grandeur and glory, what triumphs of power unbounded, what monuments of loving-kindness no less infinite!

And let it be remembered that with the greatest telescope we only see one portion of boundless space. Yes: these universes which are shown to us brightly or dimly, are still but a part of the Almighty's works. There must be more beyond, for space *is infinite.*

As we think of this, and stand in the calm lustre of the stars, while they glitter with the same radiance which kindled the inspired Psalmist's song, well may we exclaim, "When I *consider* thy heavens, the work of thy fingers, what is man that thou art mindful of him, or the son of man that thou visitest him?"

That thou visitest him! Here indeed we do know something of a thing the angels desire to look into. *He visited us;* He "who is the image of the invisible God," "by whom also He made the worlds," once took our nature upon him, and suffered for our salvation.

* La Place.

This we know, and we know the will of God concerning us, and though we can make no return for His goodness, He has graciously revealed to us how we may please Him here, and know Him more fully hereafter.

Hereafter, perhaps, we may find that the benefits of our Saviour's visit to this earth, did, in some way at present inconceivable to us, extend to distant worlds. Hereafter it may be our happiness to explore the distant parts of creation, and understand their wonders in a way of which we are now incapable.

Meanwhile, let us wait in filial confidence for the dawning of that Eternal day; assured that He who even in this life bestows so much upon His servants, is preparing for them in the "many mansions" of his house happiness such as it hath not entered into the heart of man to conceive.

> Our Friend, our Father! on Thy love we rest
>   In this our being's feeble infancy;
> By all Thy glory dazzled and oppress'd,
>   Helpless, yet strong if we are dear to Thee;
> Erring and vile, but contrite and forgiven,
> Ransomed from endless death, inheritors of heaven!
>
> Oh! may we serve Thee in our lowly sphere
>   Of Faith and Duty through Life's transient day;
> Waiting in humble hope Thy call to hear,
>   And gladly cast our childish things away,
> To see Thy face, to dwell before Thy throne,
> And Thee and these thy works, to "know as we are known!"

J. M.

INDEX.

	PAGE
Aërolites	116
Albireo	141
Aldebaran	129
Almanack, use of the	17
Arcturus, derivation of name	128
Aurora Borealis	116
Baily's Beads	57
Beer and Mädler's Map	37
Biela's Comet, separation of	97
Castor	141
Chi Cygni	133
Clusters of stars	143
Comet, Donati's	103
Comets of 1811, 1835, 1843, 1853, and 1854	100, 103
——— their great number	92
——— usual form of	93
——— of short period	96
Copernicus represented the planetary orbits circular	73
Copernicus said to have predicted the discovery of the phases of Venus	63
Corona in total solar eclipse	57
Declination	18
Delta Cephei	135
Distance of Sun, how found	25, 65
Double Stars	137
Earth is a globe	33
——— reflection of the	29
Eclipse of Moon	51
——— of Sun	50

	PAGE
Eclipses, prediction of	52
——— of Jupiter's satellites	81
Ecliptic, position of the	13
Ellipses, method of describing	75
Encke's Comet	97
Epsilon Lyræ	140
Faculæ on the Sun	24
Galileo discovered solar spots	26
Galileo, experiments of	82
——— supposed Saturn to be triple	90
Gamma Virginis	142
Globe, circumnavigation of the	34
Halley predicts a comet's return	94
Herschel, Sir William, observations by	72, 86, 137, 146
——— Sir John, opinion of, concerning the comet of 1843	102
Horizon line at sea	33
Huygens, enigma of	90
——— nebula in Orion discovered by	145
——— ring of Saturn explained by	90
Hyades, the	144
Jupiter, belts of	79
——— satellites of, discovered by Galileo	77
——— ——— eclipses of	81

Index.

	PAGE
Kepler, investigations of	74
Libration	37
Light of the Sun	27
——— three years travelling to us from a star	127
——— velocity of	84
Longitudes, lunar method of.	44
Lunar volcanos	38
Magnitudes of stars	130
Mars, appearance like snow at poles of	72
——— best known next to the Moon	71
Mercury, crescent form of	59
——— how to find	61
——— transits of	64
Meteoric stones	119
Meteors	116
Milky Way, the	147
Mira, the Wonderful Star	132
Mizar and Alcor	140
Moon, bright spots on	39
——— distance of	48
——— Earth as seen from	43
——— mountains of the	40
——— Mr. Nasmyth's observations of	39, 42
——— seasons and climate of	44
——— smooth outline of the	40
——— turns nearly the same side constantly towards the Earth	37
Nebulæ	143
Newton	31
North Polar Distance	18
Occultations	20
Orion, nebula in	145
Planets, five visible at once	17
——— variations in the apparent size of	20
Planisphere	4
Pleiades, the	143

	PAGE
Præsepe	144
Ras Algethi	145
Red prominences during total solar eclipse	57
Right Ascension	17
Roemer, discovery of	83
Satellites of Jupiter	77
——— of Saturn	86
Saturn, belts of	88
——— bright rings of	86
——— dark ring of	91
Screen, Sun's disc exhibited on a	24
Shooting Stars	116
Sirius	128
Solar spots, changes in	23
——— immense size of	26
Stars and planets strikingly different as viewed through telescope	3, 122
Stars, circumpolar	7
——— coloured	127
——— inconceivable distance of the	126
——— motion of the	122
Stars have no discs visible	123
Sun, diameter of the	49
——— precautions in observing the	22
Tails of comets, their extraordinary tenuity	110
Total solar eclipse rare in any one place	52
Tycho Brahe	31, 74
Variable Stars	131
Venus casts a shadow	69
——— crescent form of	59
——— difficulty of observing	59
——— transits of	64
——— visible in daylight	69
Zodiac, path of the planets	13
——— path of the Sun	13

WITH COLOURED PLATES.

VALUABLE WORK OF REFERENCE FOR THE GARDEN AND GREENHOUSE.

THE FLORAL WORLD
AND GARDEN GUIDE.

Edited by **SHIRLEY HIBBERD**, Esq., F.R.H.S.

Each Part contains a Coloured Illustration.

PUBLISHED MONTHLY, PRICE SIXPENCE.

Annual Subscription, Six Shillings.

A Specimen Number sent post-free for Seven Stamps.

"This very useful publication contains a vast amount of information on Horticultural matters, applicable to the wants of all sorts of gardens from the smallest to the most extensive."—*Hereford Journal.*

"We know of no serial of this character that we could recommend in priority to THE FLORAL WORLD. It is cleverly edited, and imparts a large amount of every useful information."—*Royal Cornwall Gazette.*

"If any one loves flowers, and who does not? here is a periodical to his heart's content. Every number reveals new varieties and new secrets in the horticultural art, and thereby affords the strongest evidence of its claims to public support."—*Gateshead Observer.*

"The information contained in this carefully conducted Magazine is vast, and is given with that regard to immediate utility which makes it all the more valuable."—*Coleraine Chronicle.*

"This is a very useful garden guide. For the gardener this is a very useful and well-edited publication.—*Doncaster Gazette.*

"All the information that is necessary to enable a garden or a conservatory to be duly taken care of will be found in its pages, and this is the faintest praise we can bestow upon it."—*London Mirror.*

"This admirable work—one of the best and most useful guides to the garden, and to hothouse and greenhouse management, which has been projected."—*Derby Telegraph.*

A NEW SERIES COMMENCED JANUARY 1, 1869.

Crown 8vo, elegantly bound, gilt edges, Illustrated with 12 beautifully
Coloured Engravings, price 3s. 6d., post free.

THE CANARY

Its VARIETIES, MANAGEMENT, and BREEDING;

With Portraits of the Author's own Birds.

By THE REV. FRANCIS SMITH.

Contains descriptions of all the Different Varieties of this popular Household Favourite, Illustrated with Coloured Portraits of Birds in the possession of the Author. With this book every care has been taken to produce the most Complete Manual; while the Illustrations, general appearance of the volume, and low price at which it is issued, will render it the most popular work on the subject.

CONTENTS.

A PLEA FOR THE CANARY
ORIGIN OF OUR OWN CANARIA
THE WILD CANARY
OUR LIZARDS
OUR YORKSHIRE SPANGLES
OUR NORWICH YELLOWS
OUR LONDON FANCY BIRDS
OUR BELGIANS
OUR GREEN BIRDS

OUR CINNAMONS
OUR TURNCRESTS
THE DOMINIE AND THE GERMANS
PREPARATIONS FOR BREEDING
NEST BOXES AND NESTS
OUR FIRST BIRDS
OUR MISFORTUNES
OUR INFIRMARY
ON CAGES

Opinions of the Press.

"To the reverend gentleman who gives us this book we owe much; it is so admirably done as to be thoroughly perfect as far as the subject goes. He tells us everything about the canary, and in the pleasantest manner, enlivening his story with many anecdotes. It is written in a tender and loving spirit; lucky are the birds who have so sympathetic and considerate a master, and fortunate is the master who owns so many beautiful birds; for the charming pictures that decorate the volume are so many portraits of '*the author's own pets.*' Mr. Smith is not a writer who has produced a book 'to order;' he has obviously loved his task. Years of thought and study, and familiarity with his subject in all its bearings, have enabled him to tell us everything needful to be known by those who keep the bird—one or many; how best to be its friend and its doctor; how to improve without impairing nature; how, in a word, the extremest amount of enjoyment may be derived from the cultivation of those delicious little inmates of our homes. The book is a delightful book; it may give pleasure to those who do not keep the birds; but to those who do it will be indispensable."—*Art Journal.*

"A tasteful little book, written evidently by an enthusiast in the study of the beautiful and innocent creatures whose habits he describes. It is likely to make the canary a greater favourite than ever."—*Morning Star.*

"A large amount of pleasure combined with much curious information, may be easily enjoyed by families or young folks who choose to follow Mr. Smith's directions. The book is written in a pleasing style, and will take its place as a popular manual and an ornament for the drawing-room table."—*The Student.*

"The style in which the author details the various incidents connected with his little pets is so pleasant and so alluring, that really one feels inclined on laying down the book to rush out forthwith to the nearest dealer, and without delay secure the necessary material for the formation of an aviary."—*City Press.*

"This volume contains matter valuable to all who are interested in its subject; while to those who have never paid attention to the canary the work can hardly fail to open up a source of attraction. The reverend author is an enthusiastic lover of the bird, and the result of his experience should find favour with all who share his enthusiasm."—*Glasgow Herald.*

GROOMBRIDGE AND SONS, 5, PATERNOSTER ROW, LONDON.

www.ingramcontent.com/pod-product-compliance
Lightning Source LLC
Chambersburg PA
CBHW020304170426
43202CB00008B/489